BOB FINGERMAN'S

FROM THE ASHES

[A SPECULATIVE MEMOIR]

IDW PUBLISHING

www.idwpublishing.com
ISBN: 978-160010-600-2 • 13 12 11 10 1 2 3 4

FROM THE ASHES

A Speculative Graphic Memoir
by
Bob Fingerman

EDITED by SCOTT DUNBIER

Foreword

Bob Fingerman is an irritable, negative, whiny, but very talented man who I have had the pleasure (for the most part) of knowing for many years. I usually try to avoid him, but recently he asked me to have a "nosh" with him. We caught up and he cornered me into writing this foreword. He said he felt ***From the Ashes*** was the best work he'd ever done. So, I was honored to be asked. I think I paid for the "nosh." No matter.

From the Ashes is a very personal journey that begins in an all-too-possible alternate reality in which NYC is devastated by something bad and nuclear in 2008. Bob and his wife Michele survive the bad thing and live to trek through the smoking wreckage of the city they love. They wander through many hearts of darkness to find empathy, tolerance and leather pants.

I don't think about the end of the world much. I keep my dread close and practical. Fingerman is a different specimen. If you've imagined the worst thing that can happen is an apocalyptic mess of an end to all that we know, then you are limiting yourself. In Bob's world (or end of world), it can get worse. Much worse. The horribly funny thing is you might grow to enjoy what's worse out of necessity. That is what makes human beings so wonderful and awful. They can adapt to just about anything and claim it's okay. That's called survival instinct or ignorance, depending on the situation. In ***From the Ashes*** it's both and it's funny.

Here's the kicker: everything that you think is wrong with culture, politics and people survives the end of the world. I don't want to be a spoiler but in this tight volume you will encounter:

Cannibals, zombies, mutants, religious fanatics, genderless Karl Rove clones, a human breeding farm and a kid with a labia-like neck. In these pages there are riffs on: Fox News, gender politics, Todd Browning's ***Freaks***, Anthony Bourdain and the joy of having a tail. That's to name a few.

Note: David Cross actually paid for the nosh.

One of the highlights for me happens when Bob and Michele come upon a horde of people eating other people—within days of the explosion! Not out of any kind of necessity, but because they could—this is what freedom looks like when it becomes malignant. The worst of us get worse and the best of us are baffled and amazed that the worst have no moral barometer whatsoever and if they do, its dial is spinning and the valve is hissing steam.

I'm no comic-book nerd. I've done my time with a few titles at different points in my life, but my young brain was wired by ***MAD*** magazine. Fingerman brings the same kind of vitality to the page through pen and ink that Jack Davis did—caricature that bends reality with just enough exaggeration to reveal the gooey human center with more clarity than a paragraph of prose or a photograph. His lines are forgiving because they embrace the subjects he c reates—good and bad ones—and reveal their bare humanity, which is what is at the core of all good comedy and satire.

As I said before, Fingerman is a difficult little man. He has a couple of things going for him—a very tolerant wife and a slightly irradiated heart of gold. As he and Michele trudge through the wasteland that was NYC and all else that the end of the world brings, they don't panic and they don't act out of fear. They make do and they fight the good fight. They are insulated in their love for each other and it is strong enough to bear the brunt of the apocalypse and make the best of it. That's the human spirit!

— Marc Maron
Somewhere between
New York and California,
November 2009

Marc Maron is a stand-up comic, author, feral cat wrangler and Jew. He hosts the popular podcast *WTF with Marc Maron.*

To anyone reading this book who's familiar at all with my other books, it should come as no surprise that I dedicate this one to my co-star, my wife, my true love, Michele. This book—more than any other I've done—wouldn't exist without her. I don't wish for the apocalypse (well, not *too* often), but if it does come it would be bearable with her by my side.

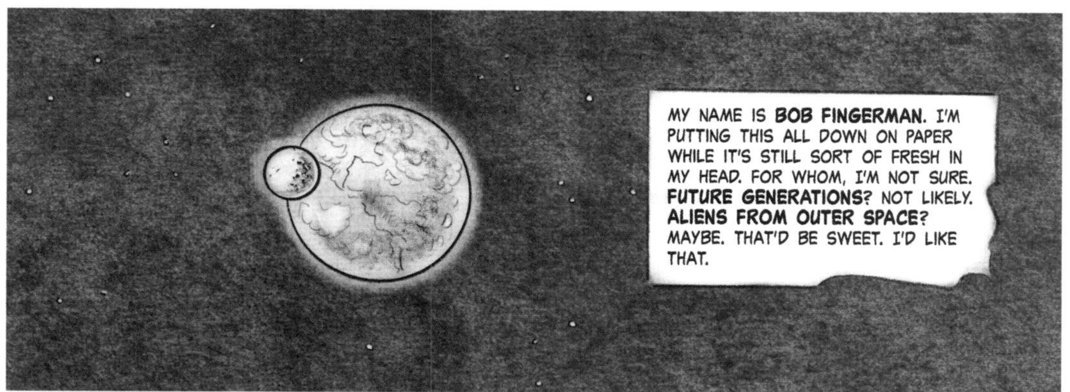
MY NAME IS **BOB FINGERMAN.** I'M PUTTING THIS ALL DOWN ON PAPER WHILE IT'S STILL SORT OF FRESH IN MY HEAD. FOR WHOM, I'M NOT SURE. **FUTURE GENERATIONS?** NOT LIKELY. **ALIENS FROM OUTER SPACE?** MAYBE. THAT'D BE SWEET. I'D LIKE THAT.

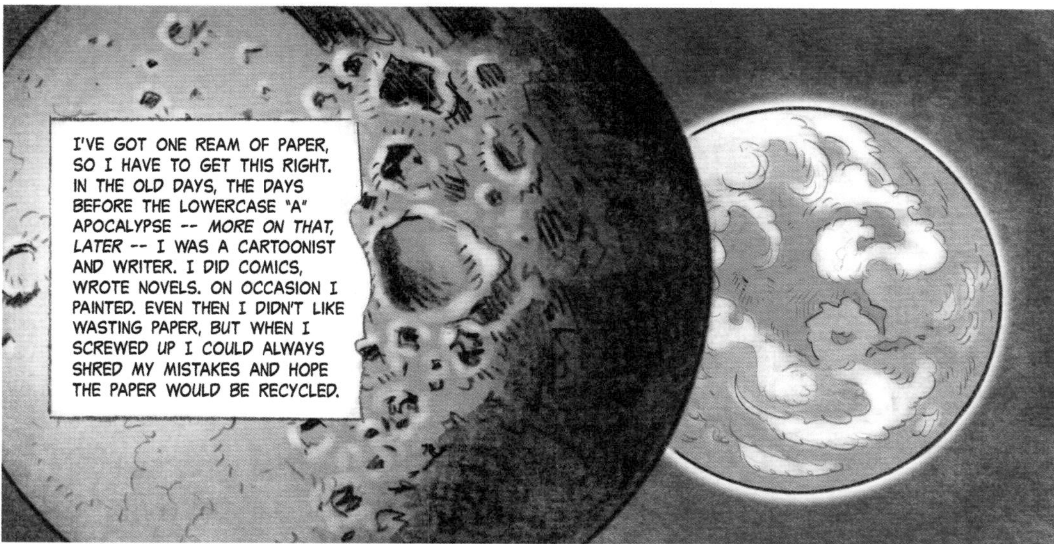
I'VE GOT ONE REAM OF PAPER, SO I HAVE TO GET THIS RIGHT. IN THE OLD DAYS, THE DAYS BEFORE THE LOWERCASE "A" APOCALYPSE -- *MORE ON THAT, LATER* -- I WAS A CARTOONIST AND WRITER. I DID COMICS, WROTE NOVELS. ON OCCASION I PAINTED. EVEN THEN I DIDN'T LIKE WASTING PAPER, BUT WHEN I SCREWED UP I COULD ALWAYS SHRED MY MISTAKES AND HOPE THE PAPER WOULD BE RECYCLED.

WELL, NO RECYCLING ANY MORE. AND CERTAINLY NO PAPER MILLS. SO, I'VE GOT ONE REAM OF COPY PAPER TO PUT THIS ALL DOWN. NOT TOO MUCH PRESSURE. BUT THEN AGAIN, LIKE I SAID, **WHO'S** GONNA READ THIS? WELL, MAYBE **YOU** WILL. YOU, **WHOEVER** YOU ARE.

THERE'S THE **IMPOSSIBLE** AND THE **IMPROBABLE** AND THIS IS CERTAINLY A TALE OF IMPROBABILITY. THAT MY WIFE, MICHELE -- THE ABSOLUTE LOVE OF MY LIFE -- AND MYSELF WERE SOMEHOW SPARED OBLITERATION WAS, WELL, ***IMPROBABLE***. BUT THERE WE WERE, INEXPLICABLY UNSCATHED, MOMENTS AFTER IT ALL WENT DOWN.
SEPTEMBER 17, 2008.
HUH.
"HUH" WHAT?
JUST "HUH." LOOK AROUND. ***THAT'S*** WHAT I MEAN. WHAT ARE THE WORDS? I'M REALLY TORN. THE SO-CALLED CIVILIZED WORLD HAS JUST BEEN PRETTY MUCH OBLITERATED, SO I GUESS I SHOULD BE BUMMED OUT.
BUT?
BUT I'M NOT. I DON'T WANNA SOUND LIKE A DICK, BUT I'M FEELING A REAL SENSE OF VINDICATION HERE. I MEAN HOW MANY YEARS HAVE I BEEN SAYING THE RELIGIOUS ZANIES WOULD DO THIS?
A LOT. ASSUMING IT WAS THEM, OF COURSE.

EXACTLY. AND YET BOOM: HERE WE ARE, APPARENTLY INTACT. MAYBE WE'RE RIDDLED WITH CANCERS AND RADIOACTIVE HOODOO, BUT WE'RE STILL STANDING.
JUST LIKE ELTON JOHN.
EXACTLY. JUST LIKE SIR ELTON FUCKING JOHN.
PROVIDED HE'S STILL STANDING, OF COURSE. AND YOU KNOW WHAT ELSE IS CHEERING ME UP?
WHAT?
LOOK: THE SMOKING CORPSE OF THE DOUCHE DOWNSTAIRS. NOW THE LOSER DOESN'T HAVE TO GO OUTSIDE TO SMOKE. EVERYTHING IS OUTSIDE. AND SMOKING.
C'MON, BOB, DON'T GLOAT.
WHAT'S THE FUN OF BEING THE SOLE SURVIVORS IF YOU CAN'T GLOAT A LITTLE?
THIS IS PRETTY AMAZING.
I KIND OF FIGURED IF THIS EVER HAPPENED I'D JUST BE VAPORIZED. I CERTAINLY DIDN'T EXPECT TO BE STROLLING AROUND.
YEAH. IT'S KIND OF WEIRD. I SHOULD BE DEVASTATED, LIKE ALL THIS. INSTEAD I FEEL SORT OF, I DUNNO, UNBURDENED. I DON'T HAVE TO GO TO WORK TODAY. OR TOMORROW. OR EVER AGAIN.

HOLY SHIT. I'M **FREE**.
SMACK!
I ACTUALLY FEEL GOOD. HAPPY. OPTIMISTIC, EVEN.
DON'T GET YOUR HOPES UP.
YOU THINK WE'RE THE LAST TWO PEOPLE ALIVE?
THAT'S **AWFUL**. I DON'T WANT EVERYONE ELSE TO BE **DEAD**. THAT'S A LITTLE EXTREME.
I KNOW. BUT **YOU'RE** STILL HERE AND AS FAR AS **I'M** CONCERNED, THAT'S ALL I NEED. YOU AND ME. THAT'S PARADISE.
TRASH
TRASH

AWWW. HOW SWEET. YOU HAVE A FUNNY IDEA OF EDEN.
WE'RE LIKE ADAM AND EVE, ONLY **STERILE**.
YOU'RE THE ONE WITH THE **VASECTOMY**.
AND YOU THINK ABSORBING A GAZILLION RADS OF NUCLEAR BLAST HAS MADE YOU A FERTILITY GODDESS? WHATEVER. WHAT'S IT MATTER? WE NEVER WANTED KIDS AND THERE'S NO ONUS ON US TO REPOPULATE.
LIKE I SAID, **PARADISE**, ONLY WITHOUT ALL THE THEISTIC BAGGAGE. WE'RE THE **OMEGA DUO**, BABY.
TRASH
JESUS, I'D HOPED YOUR BLACKBERRY HAD BEEN WIPED OUT ALONG WITH EVERYTHING ELSE. YOU EXPECT TO GET A SIGNAL?
YOU NEVER KNOW. I WANNA SEE IF ANYONE WE KNOW IS STILL ALIVE. I'M SURE YOU DON'T WANT **EVERY-ONE** WE KNOW TO BE **DEAD**.
ANYWAY, RELAX. THERE'S NO SIGNAL. IT WON'T EVEN TURN ON. IT'S DEAD. **HAPPY?**
REGARDING THE BLACKBERRY, **YES**. REGARDING EVERYONE WE KNOW, NOT SO MUCH. I SEE YOU WHIP OUT YOUR BLACKBERRY AND I HAVE A PAVLOVIAN REACTION. EVEN LOOKING OUT AT A FLATTENED HORIZON, I ***STILL*** EXPECT TO SEE YOU START WORKING.
NO. NO, NO. LIKE I SAID: **FREE**. I'M NOT RENEGING ON THAT

GOOD. SO. WHAT DO YOU WANNA DO? I SUPPOSE WE'RE GOING TO HAVE TO FIGURE OUT SOME KIND OF FOOD/SHELTER ARRANGEMENT. LOOKS LIKE MOST OF THE BUILDINGS HAVE TAKEN A BEATING.
IF BY **MOST** YOU MEAN **ALL**, AGREED. LET'S JUST WALK AND SEE WHAT WE SEE. WE ALWAYS DISCOVER NEW THINGS WHEN WE TAKE WALKS TOGETHER.
FALL'S COMING. WE SHOULD WRANGLE SOME NUCLEAR WINTER JACKETS. ALTHOUGH, WITH GLOBAL WARMING...
WHAT? WHAT'S THE MATTER?
SAKS IS GONE. AND JIMMY CHOO. OH **GOD**, THAT SOUNDS **SO** SUPERFICIAL.
NO IT DOESN'T. YOU LOVE WHAT YOU LOVE. WELL, MAYBE A LITTLE.
YEAH. ANYWAY, THIS TERRAIN ISN'T EXACTLY "HEELS FRIENDLY." I GUESS IT'S GOOD IT ALL WENT DOWN ON A **DOC MARTENS** DAY.
POST-APOCALYPTIC PRODUCT PLACEMENT.

THIS IS INTENSE.
REMEMBER THOSE COMMERCIALS FOR THAT BOARD GAME, STAY ALIVE? THE TAG LINE WAS, "I'M THE SOLE SURVIVOR!"
NO. PROBABLY BEFORE MY TIME.
LISTEN, LITTLE MISS CHILD BRIDE, NOT EVERYTHING I REMEMBER IS BEFORE YOUR TIME. IT WAS FROM THE LATE SEVENTIES. IF YOUR MARBLES DIDN'T FALL THROUGH THE HOLES YOU WERE "THE SOLE SURVIVOR."
TRASH
OH YEAAAH. "I'M THE SOLE SURVIVOR!" NOW I REMEMBER. I THINK I MIGHT HAVE HAD THAT GAME.
SIGH SEE? ANYWAY, THAT'S US. WE'RE THE SOLE SURVIVORS, I THINK.
THAT'S CRAZY. THERE HAS TO BE SOMEONE ELSE.

IF POST-APOC' MOVIES ARE ANY INDICATION, WE CAN EXPECT MUTANTS, SOUPED-UP CARS AND BIKERS WEARING FETISH-GEAR AND CUT-UP TIRE SHOULDER-PADS.
BECAUSE REAL LIFE IS **JUST** LIKE THE MOVIES.
EXACTLY. AND I'D BETTER NOT BREAK MY GLASSES. I DON'T WANT SOME MAUDLIN BURGESS MEREDITH SCENE.
THAT REMINDS ME I NEED CONTACT LENS SOLUTION. LET'S HIT THE REMAINS OF A **DUANE READE** AND LOOT.
WELL, THIS IS GRIM.
ON THE PLUS SIDE, AT LEAST THERE ARE NO LINES.

FIND WHAT YOU NEEDED?
YEAH. I'M GONNA FILL MY BAG. WHO KNOWS WHEN WE'LL COME ACROSS MORE OF THIS STUFF? YOU GRAB-BING ANYTHING?
YEAH. SOME ASTROGLIDE.
ONE-TRACK MIND.
YOU HAVE YOUR PRIORITIES, I HAVE MINE. THAT AND EARPLUGS.
BECAUSE THINGS ARE SO NOISY NOW.
GOOD POINT.
I TAKE IT BACK: YOU **ARE** MY CHILD BRIDE. **ONLY** A CHILD BRIDE COULD GET AWAY WITH ***THAT*** KNAPSACK.
IT'S **CUTE**. AND IT'S ALL THERE WAS.

I MANAGED TO FIND **THIS**.
YOU STOLE IT OFF A **CORPSE**. I WANTED BAGGAGE WITH NO BAGGAGE.
FAIR ENOUGH. ANYWAY, THERE'S STILL A DUANE READE ON EVERY CORNER.
AND AT LEAST THREE BANKS. ONLY NOW THEY'RE TRASHED.
YOU DON'T SEE ME CRYING.
TRASH
I SNAGGED SOME EDIBLES, TOO. SOME ENTENMANN'S THAT WASN'T GLOWING AND SOME SLIM JIMS.
WERE ***THEY*** GLOWING?
I **THINK** THEY WERE SLIM JIMS. MAYBE THEY WERE GLOW-STICKS.
BROADWAY
NOT EXACTLY GOURMET. GLOW-STICKS COULDN'T TASTE MUCH WORSE THAN THIS.
OR HAVE LESS NUTRITION. STILL, BEATS STARVING. DID YOU TAKE ANY **GUM**?
SADLY, NO. SORRY.
WE'RE GOING TO BE **AFTER**-TASTING THESE SLIM JIMS ALL NIGHT.
TRASH

WE'LL FORAGE IN A SUPERMARKET TOMORROW. **GATORADE**?
I S'POSE. WHY'D YOU TAKE GATORADE INSTEAD OF WATER? WE BOTH ***HATE*** IT.
IT'S GOT ELECTRO-LYTES?
WHICH ARE?
I DUNNO, BUT IT'S THE POST-APOCALYPSE, SO I'M SURE WE NEED 'EM. ANYWAY, WHAT DO YOU WANNA DO NOW?

PUT THAT ASTROGLIDE TO GOOD USE?
OUT HERE IN THE OPEN?
WHO'S GONNA SEE?
TRASH

'MORNING. UGH. MY MOUTH TASTES LIKE SOMETHING USED IT AS A TOILET, WIPED ITS ASS WITH A BIGGER, SMELLIER ASS, THEN USED IT AGAIN AND FORGOT TO FLUSH.
MINE TOO. SLIM JIMS, CHOCOLATE POP 'EMS AND ONLY GATORADE TO RINSE WITH. ICK.
OY. OKAY, SO TODAY WE FIND WATER AND REAL FOOD. AND LISTERINE. AND A CAN OPENER.
I'LL MAKE A LIST.
I'M A 'TARD. I WAS JUST REACHING FOR MY BLACKBERRY. YOU HAVE ANY PAPER?
NOPE.
AN ARTIST WITH NO PAPER.
I KNOW, PATHETIC. OKAY, SO TODAY WE'LL TRY TO ROUND UP SOME ESSENTIALS. YESTERDAY WAS, "HOLY SHIT, WE'RE ALIVE DAY," BUT TODAY'S "LET'S GET SERIOUS AND BE PREPARED DAY."
AMEN. SPEAKING OF NO PAPER AND TOILETS, WE NEED TO GET SOME MOIST BUTT-WIPES, TOO. IT'S NOT LIKE WE CAN SHOWER.
YEAH. APOCALYPSE OR NO, I NEED A CLEAN PO-PO. I DON'T WANNA END UP AS THE 'ROID WARRIOR. AS REDD FOXX SAID: "YOU GOTTA WASH YO' ASS."
IF TODAY'S "LET'S GET SERIOUS AND BE PREPARED DAY," LET'S ASSUME TOMORROW WILL BE "OH GOD, IT'S HITTING ME LIKE A TON OF BRICKS THAT WE MADE IT AND CHANCES ARE OUR LOVED ONES ARE DEAD DAY."

≥SIGH≤ IF WE THINK ABOUT ALL OUR DEAD FRIENDS AND FAMILY WE'LL CURL UP IN FETAL POSITIONS NEVER TO RISE AGAIN. GOTTA KEEP MOVING.
I REMEMBER THIS TV MOVIE WITH ED ASNER AND SALLY STRUTHERS CRASH-LANDED IN THE FROZEN YUKON WILDER-NESS.
AND THAT HAS WHAT TO DO WITH WHAT?
ASNER KEPT TELLING HER TO KEEP MOVING TO STAY ALIVE. SO, THAT'S WHAT **WE'RE** GONNA DO.
AH.
I ALSO REMEMBER IT WAS KINDA BORING. BUT THEY NEVER RESORTED TO **CANNIBALISM**.
I SUPPOSE THAT'S WORTH SOMETHING.
TRASH
YES. LET'S VOW TO HONOR THE *ASNER-STRUTHERS PACT OF '75* AND **NOT** EAT ANY PEOPLE, NO MATTER HOW *DELICIOUS* THEIR ROASTED FLESH SMELLS.
AMEN.
I REALLY AM GLAD YOUR BLACKBERRY IS DEAD.
I KNOW.
TRASH

I SUPPOSE, AT THIS POINT, IT WOULD BEHOOVE ME TO GIVE YOU A LITTLE BACKGROUND ON OUR LIVES *BEFORE* THE HOLOCAUST. IT MIGHT HELP PUT CERTAIN THINGS IN PERSPECTIVE. I SHOULD ALSO MENTION -- SO THAT *YOU* DON'T THINK MICHELE AND I HEARTLESS MONSTERS -- THAT WE DID IN FACT RUMINATE ON OUR LOST LOVED ONES AND LO AND BEHOLD DID CURL INTO FETAL POSITIONS, MEWLING IN ABJECT GRIEF. IT WASN'T PRETTY AND IT LASTED FOR TWO FULL DAYS. TO KEEP THINGS BREEZY -- *OR AT LEAST AS BREEZY AS A STORY LIKE THIS CAN BE* -- I CHOSE TO SKIP PAST THAT EPISODE AND GET ON WITH THINGS. ANYWAY, LET'S TAKE A BRIEF LOOK AT OUR LIVES, PRE-ARMAGEDDON.

...**I DON'T UNDERSTAND!** I'M **GOOD** TO YOU. I'M **ALWAYS** GOOD TO **YOU!** WHY ARE YOU **DOING** THIS TO ME? WHAT THE **FUCK** HAVE I **EVER** DONE TO YOU TO DESERVE **THIS SHIT?**

YOU'RE SUCH A HATEFUL BITCH, YOU REALLY ARE!

AND... CRASH. PREDICTABLE. YOU ARE SUCH A FUCKING MISERY. YOU REALLY ARE. I HOPE A SANTA ANA OF AIRBORNE, FAST-ACTING AIDS, BLASTS THE MICRO-SOFT COMPOUND AND ANNIHILATES IT.

I DON'T GET IT. I REALLY DON'T. NEW COMPUTER, OLD COMPUTER. IT'S ALL THE SAME. PCs **SUCK**. SOMEDAY I'LL HEMORRHAGE THE LOOT AND GET A MAC.
GEEZ, IF ANYONE HEARS THESE TIRADES THEY MUST THINK I'M ABUSING MICHELE.
AND AS I WAGED COMBAT WITH MY PC -- AND *PERPETUALLY LOST* -- MICHELE, THE DIRECTOR OF HUMAN RESOURCES FOR ***GELDBILDETGELDBANK***, A MULTINATIONAL MEGA-INVESTMENT BANK, HAD IT COMING AT HER FROM ALL DIRECTIONS.
I REALLY DON'T THINK WE NEED TO GUARANTEE HIM **ANYTHING**. IT'S NOT LIKE THERE ARE A TON OF JOBS OUT THERE. I'LL MAKE THE OFFER AND GET BACK TO YOU. **BYE**.
⋛SIGH⋚ WOULD IT BE ASKING TOO MUCH TO GET SOME LUNCH IN PEACE?
BREEP-BREEP!
APPARENTLY IT WOULD.
THIS IS MICHELE. YES, I UNDERSTAND. YES, SHE KNOWS ABOUT THE SITUATION. ***NO***, IT'S NOT YET RESOLVED. ***DAVID***, I'LL BE BACK IN THE OFFICE SOON. RIGHT. **BYE**.
BREEP-BREEP!
⋛SIGH⋚
⋛PHEW⋚ HI, SWEETIE.

HI. I TRIED UPSTAIRS AND THEY SAID YOU'D LEFT FOR LUNCH. I'M AMAZED YOU ACTUALLY GOT OUT. OH. A WHOLE THREE FEET FROM THE BUILDING. NICE. YOU SHOULD JUST TURN YOUR BLACKBERRY OFF. I KNOW. TURN IT OFF, ANYWAY. I KNOW, WISHFUL THINKING.
YOU AND ME BOTH. I'D LOVE TO TALK, BUT I HAVE TO GET SOMETHING TO EAT.
LISTEN, SWEETIE, I'M NOT SURE I'LL BE HOME FOR DINNER TONIGHT. IT MIGHT BE A LATE ONE. I'LL LET YOU KNOW. LOVE YOU. BYE.
BREEP-BREEP!
UCCH
HI. OKAY, SO DID --
AND AS MICHELE INCHED HER WAY TOWARDS LUNCH, I RESUMED HOSTILITIES WITH MY ASSHOLISH COMPUTER...
FINE, CRASH AGAIN. I'LL DO A SYSTEM RESTORE FOR THE THOUSANDTH TIME, YOU CRUEL PRICK. WANT ME TO PROSTRATE MYSELF BEFORE YOU? TO BEG YOU TO WORK?
I CAN'T GIVE YOU THAT. MY SELF-ESTEEM -- SUCH AS IT IS -- WON'T LET ME KNEEL BEFORE A MACHINE. FUCK YOU. I'M OUT OF HERE.

NO MORE SMALL.
≶SIGH≶ FINE. I'LL TAKE A JUMBO.
T'REE DOLLAH.
FINE. "THANKS."
OH, WILL SHORTZ, YOU THINK YOU'VE GOT ME ON THE ROPES WITH A **PUN** LIKE ***THAT***? I DON'T THINK--
GODDAMMIT. THAT'LL LEARN ME TO TRY AND RELAX.
SPLOP!

BREET-BREET!
I'M REALLY SORRY, I GOTTA GET THIS CALL. AS I'VE SUGGESTED BEFORE, YOU REALLY GOTTA TALK TO SUZANNE.
BREET-BREET!
BUT, I REALLY KNOW THAT YOU CAN REALLY GET THIS DONE, WHICH IS REALLY WHY I CAME TO YOU, BECAUSE, REALLY--
PARRISH
BREET-BREET!
DUDE, I REALLY NEED TO TAKE THIS CALL.
BUT I-- O-KAAAAY.
HEY, BRUCE, I THINK WE HAVE A PROBLEM. WE GOT THE REFERENCE CHECK BACK ON JOHN KRISCZINSKI AND THEY'RE TELLING US HE NEVER WORKED AT SILVERGOLDENBERG BROTHERS. WELL, HE TOTALLY FALSIFIED THE PAY STUB. YEAH, WE GOTTA FIRE HIM. RIGHT, I GOTTA FIRE HIM.
OH, HEY, JOHN, HOW'S IT GOING? UM, HAVE A SEAT.

AM I FIRED? PLEASE DON'T TELL ME I'M FIRED. I CAN'T LOSE THIS JOB. I NEED THIS JOB.
OH, GOD, I'M FIRED, AREN'T I? I KNEW IT. I FUCKING KNEW IT. OH, GOD, OH JESUS. AM I FIRED?
I--
YOU KNOW WHAT? WHO NEEDS THIS JOB? I'M A YOUNG DYNAMO. IF GELDBILDET-GELDBANK CAN'T RECOGNIZE THAT--
JOHN--
PLEASE DON'T FIRE ME! PLEEEAAASE!
LATER...
ALONE AT LAST. FINALLY.
I KNOW. SORRY I'M LATE, BUT I COULDN'T GET A CAB.
I'M JUST HAPPY YOU'RE HERE. AND IT'S "ONLY" NINE O'CLOCK.
DON'T REMIND ME. I JUST WANT A GLASS OF WINE AND--
MENU
BZZZT-BZZZT!

AND THE FUCKING CRACKBERRY. DON'T ANSWER IT.
I HAVE TO. I'LL ONLY BE A MINUTE.
TICKA-TAP-TACK-TICK-TACK-TICKA-TAP...
UH-HUH. SOMEDAY YOU'LL BE FREE OF THAT MISERABLE THING AND THAT WILL BE THE HAPPIEST DAY OF MY LIFE.
YOU SURE YOU WANT TO DO THIS?
IT'LL BE CATHARTIC.
YOU'LL GET NO ARGUMENT FROM ME. I'VE WAITED A LONG TIME FOR THIS.
AND ALL IT TOOK TO GET HERE WAS THE END OF THE WORLD.
A SMALL PRICE TO PAY.
BYE-BYE, BLACKBERRY.
TRASH

OUCH!
THAT WAS AN "OUCH!"
I TOLD YOU WE'RE NOT ALONE.
SO MUCH FOR PARADISE.
OH, STOP! C'MON, LET'S CHECK IT OUT!
BUT IT COULD BE--
DON'T BE SUCH A PILL!
TRASH

OH MY GOD.
HUH.
"HUH"? THAT'S YOUR REACTION? "HUH"?
IF IT WAS GOOD ENOUGH FOR THE END OF THE WORLD, IT'S GOOD ENOUGH FOR THIS.

BUT THEY... THEY... THEY'VE RESORTED TO **CANNIBALISM!**
LOOKS LIKE.
IT'S ONLY BEEN A ***COUPLE OF DAYS!***
ONE SHUDDERS TO THINK HOW MANY **SECONDS** IT TOOK BEFORE THEY STARTED DRINKING THEIR OWN **URINE**.

HEY, LOOK! **PEOPLE!**
YEAH! MORE FOR THE ***FEAST!***
THEY'RE COMING THIS WAY.
OBVIOUSLY THEY'RE **NOT** SIGNATORIES OF THE ASNER-STRUTHERS PACT OF '75.
WE'RE **SO** BONED.
TRASH
AND AS THE WILD-EYED CANNIBAL HORDE APPROACHED, I SUDDENLY FELT NOSTALGIC FOR DOING BATTLE WITH MY SADISTIC COMPUTER.

STAY BACK, YOU FREAKS! YOU'RE NOT EATING ME.
NO DUH, SISTER. YOU ARE SO NOT MY TYPE.
I DON'T THINK SHE MEANT THAT DIRTIFULLY, GEO, I THINK SHE MEANT THAT LITERALLY.
TRASH
WHAT? OH, HONEY, PUH-LEEZE.
RIGHT, I'M THE CRAZY ONE. YOU GUYS ARE CHOWING DOWN ON THAT, THAT, CORPSE AND--
COULD YOU MAKE THAT SOUND LESS APPETIZING?

YOU WERE COMING RIGHT AT US. HAVE YOU GUYS TAKEN A LOOK IN THE MIRROR? YOU LOOK, UM, MENTAL?
THAT'S NICE.
YOU JUST SAID, "MORE FOR THE FEAST."
EXACTLY. COME ONE, COME ALL. THE MORE THE MERRIER. WE'RE NOT SELFISH. THERE'S PLENTY TO GO 'ROUND.
TRASH
YOU THOUGHT WE MEANT YOU WERE THE FEAST? THAT'S HILARIOUS!
FOR REALS. HAVE EITHER OF YOU GOTTEN A WHIFF OF THIS LONG PIG? IT SMELLS DIVINE.
IT'S NOT LIKE WE KILLED ANYONE. WHATEVER THEY BLASTED US WITH DID THESE FOLKS TO A FARE-THEE-WELL.
BUT THERE'S A SUPERMARKET RIGHT OVER THERE.
NO DUH. WHERE D'YA THINK WE GOT THE DIPPING SAUCE?
UGH. THEY'RE WORSE THAN CANNIBALS. THEY'RE FOODIES.
FOOD EMPOR
B-BUT... UH-UH. NO. YOU'VE RESORTED TO CANNIBALISM. THERE'S NO EXCUSE.
THAT KIND OF PROVINCIAL THINKING IS SO A FEW DAYS AGO. THE OLD TABOOS DON'T APPLY.
TRASH

WHAT DOES W.W.B.D. STAND FOR?
WHAT WOULD BOURDAIN DO?
AND IF IT WAS THE LOCAL CUISINE, THE ANSWER IS "DIG IN."
W.W.B.D.
TRASH
DID YOU IDIOTS EVEN WATCH HIS SHOW? HE WOULD NEVER EAT HUMAN. NOT EVEN IN PAPUA.
MAYBE NOT, BUT HE'S THE PLAT DU JOUR AND HE'S DELICIOUS.
I, FOR ONE, HAVE LOST MY APPETITE.
≷SNIFF-SNIFF-SNIFF≶ UGH. I CAN'T BLAME YOU. SLIM JIMS, GATORADE AND ENTENMANN'S CHOCOLATE POP 'EMS. NAUSEATING.
YOU CAN TELL THAT FROM MY BREATH?
MM-HMM.
WE ARE SO GETTING MINTS AND TOOTHPASTE, BOB.
TRASH
SPEAKING OF WHICH, IT'S BEEN REAL SWELL TALKING WITH YOU "GASTRONOMES," BUT I THINK WE'LL STICK TO NORMAL FOOD, WHAT WITH THAT SUPERMARKET THERE NOT TWENTY PACES AWAY.
SUIT YOURSELVES.
YEAH, ENJOY YOUR WONDER BREAD AND VELVEETA.
SNAP!

YEAH, WE'RE THE ONES TO MOCK. I DON'T EAT WONDER BREAD. ARNOLD, MAYBE. PEPPERIDGE FARM. CANNIBALS MAKIN' FUN OF ME--
LET IT GO, BOB. JUST BE GLAD THEY DIDN'T EAT US.
TRASH
--BUNCH OF NO-BUSINESS-BORN GHOULISH MOTHER-FUCKERS.
BOB, SERIOUSLY.
I'M GETTIN' ME SOME DINTY MOORE! THAT'S GOOD EATIN'. AND SPAM.
WON'T CATCH ME EATING MY NEIGHBORS! I LIKE ENTEN-MANN'S! HEAR THAT, YOU RUGGERO DEODATO-EMULATING FOOD SNOBS?!?
ENTENMANN'S RULES!

WHO THE HELL IS RUGGERO DEODATO?

THAT WAS A VAST IMPROVEMENT OVER THE DUANE READE HAUL.

YUP. I'M STILL EMBARRASSED THAT GUY COULD TELL WHAT I ATE FROM MY BREATH.

YOU'RE EMBARRASSED BECAUSE A **CANNIBAL** HELD YOU IN LOW ESTEEM?

IT'S STUPID, I ADMIT.

RIDICULOUS. BUT THAT'S SOME POMO CARNIE TRICK. BEATS GUESSING YOUR WEIGHT.

IF HE'D TRIED ***THAT*** I'D HAVE KICKED HIM SO HARD HIS **BALLS** WOULD HAVE SHOT OUT HIS **NOSTRILS**.

AND HIS BUDDIES WOULD'VE GOBBLED THEM UP, RIGHT QUICK. SPEAKING OF WHICH, ANY ROOM FOR "DESSERT?"

"DESSERT?" **OH**. NO, NOT TONIGHT. THAT ENCOUNTER REALLY TOOK IT OUT OF ME.

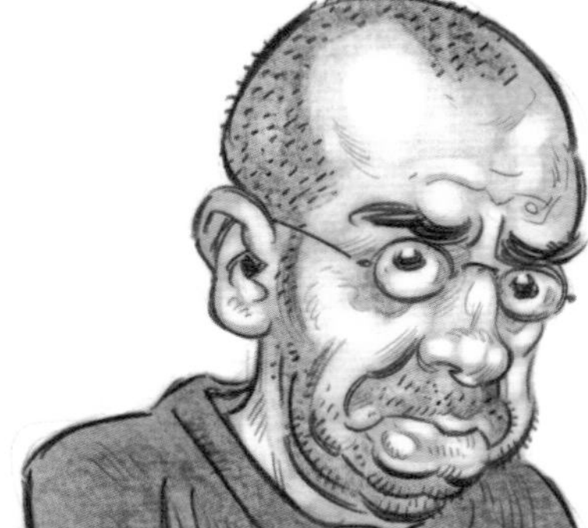

I HOPE, I HOPE, I HOPE...
OH MY GOD. THE TOILET STILL FLUSHES!
SFLOSHH!
OOH-OOH! ME NEXT!
THE TANK ISN'T REFILLING. I THINK I USED IT UP. SORRY.
WHAT DIFFERENCE DOES IT MAKE? WE'RE MOVING ON, ANYWAY. LET ME HAVE A MOMENT, THEN WE'LL SPLIT.
TRASH
I WISH THERE'D BEEN RUNNING WATER. I COULD USE A SHOWER. THAT'S ONE THING I'LL **REALLY** MISS.
WE'RE **BOTH** A LITTLE WHIFFY, I'M SURE.
YEAH, BUT ON **YOU** IT SMELLS GOOD.
THE SICK PART IS I KNOW YOU **MEAN** IT.
TRASH

West End Ave
West 79th St.
LOOK, WE'RE ON 79TH AND WEST END.
SO?
SO, THIS IS WHERE OUR DENTISTS WERE.
YOU'LL PARDON ME FOR NOT MISTING UP OVER CHOPPERS.
LOOK: THESE ARE MINE.
THAT IS ONE STRANGE ARTIFACT TO BE HAPPY TO UNEARTH.
TRASH
GOD **DAMN** IT.
WE'LL HAVE TO FIND YOU SOME NEW PANTS. **YAY!**
YOU **DON'T** HAVE TO SOUND SO **HAPPY** ABOUT IT.
BOB, THIS IS AS CLOSE TO **SHOPPING** AS I'M GOING TO GET FROM NOW ON. ALLOW ME TO BASK.
THERE WAS THAT PLACE ON COLUMBUS. LET'S HEAD SOUTH-EAST.
SHHRRRIP!
smart

WHO GETS AN "A" FOR FORAGING?
I'M NOT WEARING THOSE.
WHY NOT?
LEATHER PANTS? THEY'RE TOTALLY GAY.
BOB, HAVE YOU NOTICED THE WHOLE END OF THE WORLD THEME WE'VE GOT GOING ON HERE? WHY BE SO UPTIGHT? WAS MAD MAX GAY? YOU LIKE THE MAD MAX.
HE WAS AN ANTI-SEMITE.
MEL GIBSON WAS AN ANTI-SEMITE! MAD MAX WAS...?
MAD MAX WAS THE COOLEST.
RIGHT. NOW PUT 'EM ON.
AS LONG AS MY PANTS ARE OFF...?
IF YOU'RE A GOOD BOY AND TRY ON THE NEW ONES, MAYBE LATER WE'LL HAVE THE SEX.
TRASH

I FEEL LIKE AN IDIOT. A GAY IDIOT.
THEY HIGHLIGHT YOUR HIGH ROUND COOLIE. ME LIKEY.
I DON'T SEE YOU SPORTIN' ANY LEATHER.
IT WAS A MEN'S STORE, BOB.
A GAY MEN'S STORE.
STOP BEING A BABY. THAT WAS A REGULAR MEN'S STORE THAT SOLD REGULAR LEATHER GOODS FOR REGULAR GUYS.
BECAUSE HENRY FONDA ALWAYS WORE LEATHER PANTS.
SIGH HE DIDN'T, BUT PETER FONDA DID AND YOU THINK PETER FONDA IS WHAT?
TOTALLY COOL.
RIGHT. SO IF MAD MAX AND PETER FONDA LOOK COOL IN BLACK LEATHER PANTS...?
I DO TOO?
PRESENT WHININESS ASIDE, I FIND YOU IRRESISTIBLY DOABLE.
LEATHER PANTS IT IS.

I DON'T KNOW ABOUT THAT APPLE. IT COULD BE RADIOACTIVE.
SO COULD WE. BESIDES, DIDN'T THEY ALREADY SELL IRRADIATED PRODUCE? CONSIDER THIS SUPER-SIZED.
TUNA
WOW. THAT'S ONE BIG CHUNK OF CALAMARI.
THINK THAT GOT BLASTED ALL THE WAY FROM THE OCEAN?
AAUGH! JESUS, IT'S ALIVE!
YEEP!
TRASH
THUP!

WHATTAYA MEAN "IT'S ALIVE"? I'M NOT AN "IT." A MAN GROWS TENTACLES AND ALL OF A SUDDEN HE'S AN "IT."
PARDON THE LACK OF POKER FACE, BUT JESUS H. CHRIST.
WAY TO MAKE ME FEEL BETTER ABOUT ALL THIS, SON.
THOSE NUKEY MUTAGENS MUST'VE BEEN FASTER-ACTIN' THAN TINACTIN.
SEE, 'CAUSE THAT MAKES ME FEEL A LOT BETTER, MAKIN' JOKES AT MY EXPENSE. NO REALLY, THAT'S VERY CLEVER AND NOT AT ALL INSENSITIVE AS A SANDPAPER DILDO.
SORRY.
YOU GOT NO CAUSE TO APOLOGIZE, GIRLIE. GEORGE MICHAEL, HERE, THOUGH--
SIGH SEE? THE PANTS. I KNEW IT.
HE'S SELF-CONSCIOUS ABOUT THE PANTS.
TRASH
HE'S SELF-CONSCIOUS ABOUT THE PANTS. I'M SELF-CONSCIOUS ABOUT THE TENTACLES. THAT'S ROUGHLY EQUAL.

DON'T FORGET YOUR VAGUELY SATANIC GOAT EYES.
I'VE ONLY KNOWN YOU TWO FOR ABOUT FORTY SECONDS BUT I CAN ALREADY TELL YOU'RE THE PERFECT COUPLE.
I LIKE THIS GUY.
AND HE'S SARCASTIC.
I KNOW MY HUSBAND. HE MEANS IT.
YOU LIKE A TENTACLE-HAVIN', GOAT-EYED FREAK YOU JUST MET.
YUP.
IN THAT CASE, I'M BYRON. OKAY, COME MEET THE REST OF THE GANG.
DOWN THERE.

NICE HONEY-WAGONS.
EXCUSE ME? OH, YEAH. YEAH. THEY WERE SHOOTING SOME MOVIE.
IF YOU'RE EAGER TO MEET THE BAKED REMAINS OF WILL SMITH, NOW'S YOUR CHANCE.
HUH. EVEN IN DEATH HE'S PRETERNATURALLY LIKEABLE.
UH, I'LL PASS. IT'D BE IRONIC IF IT WAS THE SEQUEL TO I AM LEGEND.
TRASH
YUP. ANYWAY, THESE CELEB TRAILERS ARE WAY NICER THAN THOSE FORMALDEHYDE-SOAKED FEMA ONES.
SOME OF MY FAMILY LIVED IN THE NINTH WARD. TRUTH IS, THEY NEVER EVEN GOT ONE OF THOSE TOXIC TRAILERS.
WELL, WE'RE ALL IN THE SHIT NOW.
TRUE. C'MON, LET'S MEET THE OTHERS.
TRASH

GANG, THIS IS MICHELE AND BOB. THEY'RE, UH, "NORMAL."
NORMAL FOR WHAT, A VILLAGE PEOPLE COVER BAND?
THAT'S IT, THE PANTS GO. I'LL WALK AROUND BALLS OUT IF THIS IS HOW IT'S GONNA BE.
KEEP YOUR PANTS ON.
PLEASE. I'M JUST BUSTIN' YOUR HUMP, PAL.
IS THAT A CRACK AT MY EXPENSE? I THINK HE LOOKS RAD.
THE LADIES LIKE THE LEATHER PANTS.
MM-HMM. AND I KNOW YOU LIKE THOSE TATTOOED NERD-GIRLS.
(YEAH, I'M REALLY INTO JOE CAMEL AND QUASIMODO, TOO.)
(I WAS JUST KIDDING. SORT OF.)

DUDES, WELCOME TO THE MISFITS. GET IT? BECAUSE WE'RE--
YEAH, YEAH. WOW, THAT'S SOME VOICE. YOU BEEN HUFFING HELIUM?
NOT HUFFING, EXUDING. CHECK THIS OUT. GIMME A HIT, VIC.
MISFITS
SMOOOOOCHIFLATE!
WE REPRESENT THE LOLLIPOP GUILD AND IN THE NAME OF THE LOLLIPOP GUILD, WE WISH TO WELCOME YOU TO MUTANT LAND...
ADORABLE, NO?
I'M BOTH CHARMED AND TOTALLY CREEPED OUT.
IMAGINE HOW WE FEEL. THANK GOD ALL THE MIRRORS ARE GONE.
AMEN.
MISFITS

OVER THE NEXT FEW WEEKS, MICHELE AND I SETTLED IN WITH OUR NEW MUTANT PALS. OKAY, SO THEY WERE A BIT CHALLENGING ON THE EYES AT FIRST, BUT MORE SIGNIFICANTLY THEY WERE AN INTERESTING BUNCH; SMART, CAPABLE, CHATTY. GOOD COMPANY. THOUGH I'D BEEN PERFECTLY HAPPY TO BE ALONE WITH MICHELE, IT WAS NICE TO HAVE SOME NEW FRIENDS. THOUGH I'D NEVER BEEN DRAWN TO AGRARIAN LIFE, WE SOON GOT INTO THE SPIRIT OF PLANTING CROPS. ALL THE PRODUCE IN THE MARKETS WAS LONG ROTTED AND MAN -- AND MUTANT -- DOES NOT LIVE BY CANNED GOODS ALONE.
YOU MUST BE HAPPY. YOU ALWAYS HANKERED TO DO SOME GARDENING.
I **AM** HAPPY. WHO'D HAVE THOUGHT THE APOCALYPSE COULD BE SO RELAXING?
AND NOW THAT THEY SET UP THE **RAIN SHOWER**, I FEEL MORE LIKE MYSELF.
TRASH
I'VE KIND OF LOST TRACK, BUT IT MUST BE MID-OCTOBER BY NOW. IT'S STILL REALLY WARM.
THE NUKE-FEST MUST'VE REALLY SCREWED WITH THE CLIMATE. I WONDER IF WE'LL GET GIANT MUTANT VEGETABLES, LIKE IN THAT WOODY ALLEN MOVIE, **SLEEPER**.
SPEAKING OF SHOWERING, I'M **FILTHY**.
THERE'S ROOM FOR TWO.
SOUNDS GOOD.
SSNNNAAAAARRRLL
THAT'S NOT A GOOD SOUND.
NO, IT **ISN'T**.

IF I WASN'T SO TERRIFIED, THIS WOULD BE THE PERFECT OPPORTUNITY TO COMPLAIN ABOUT PEOPLE WHO PRONOUNCE **CERBERUS**, *THE HOUND OF HADES*, AS **CEREBUS**, *THE CARTOON AARDVARK.*
BUT I'M TOO TERRIFIED.
YES, IT'S CLEAR YOU'RE INCAPABLE OF BEING A KNOW-IT-ALL AT THE MOMENT.
RUN!!!
GGGRRRRRRRR

I LIKED PLAYING RESIDENT EVIL. I DIDN'T WANT TO LIVE IT.
LESS KVETCHING, MORE RUNNING!
TRASH

CAESAR, HEEL!
THAT WAS AMAZING.
AW, CAESAR'S A GOOD DOG. HE'S JUST A LITTLE CONFUSED. THREE HEADS AREN'T BETTER THAN ONE.
I DON'T MEAN TO BE RUDE, SIR, BUT ARE YOU OKAY? YOU LOOK A LITTLE...
DEAD? SEE? RESIDENT EVIL. NOW WE'VE GOT ZOMBIES.
YEAH. NOT WILD ABOUT THAT TERM. SOUNDS... DEROGATORY.

YEAH. "ZOMBIE" CONNOTES LACK OF BRAIN FUNCTION.
YEAH, AND HUMAN-FLESH-EATING. WE'RE NOT CANNIBALS.
WE ALREADY MET SOME OF THOSE.
THOSE GUYS. UGH. THE FOODIES. WE DON'T EAT ANYTHING. EVER.
THE GREAT THING ABOUT BEING UNDEAD IS IT'S AN AWESOME APPETITE SUPPRESSANT. IN THE MOVIES IT'S ALL LIKE, "EAT, EAT, EAT. MMMM: INTESTINES." I DON'T CRAVE ANYTHING. IT'S AWESOME. YOU SHOULD TOTALLY TRY IT.
IF I DIE AND COME BACK, I'LL DEFINITELY GIVE IT A WHIRL. BUT TILL THEN...
THIS IS AMAZING. WE'VE GOT MUTANTS, ZOMB-- I MEAN, UM...
WE LIKE REANIMATED-AMERICANS.
ANYWAY, YOU SHOULD COME HANG OUT WITH THE MUTANT CROWD. THEY'RE GOOD PEOPLE.
FOR MUTANTS, THEY'RE NOT TOO WILD ABOUT CAESAR.
OR ZOMBIES. UGH, NOW I'M DOING IT. OR US.
WELL, IF YOU EVER CHANGE YOUR MIND.
THANKS. WE'LL THINK ABOUT IT.

NOW I REALLY NEED A SHOWER. THAT MONSTER DOG WAS THE FINAL STRAW.
I WON'T SAY IT SCARED THE SHIT OUT OF ME, BUT IT KNOCKED A FEW FARTS LOOSE.
DITTO.
YEAH, BUT YOURS AREN'T TRAPPED INSIDE AIRTIGHT LEATHER PANTS. WHEN I REMOVE THESE IT'S GONNA BE BHOPAL ALL OVER AGAIN.
I LOVE YOU.
I'M GONNA GO GRAB THAT SHOWER.
YEAH, I--
YOU GOTTA COME CHECK THIS OUT! TROUBLE!
TRASH

QUICK, QUICK!
WE'RE COMING, WE'RE COMING!
MISFI
TRASH
THIS IS SO FUCKED UP.
LOOK AT THIS! WHAT THE HELL ARE THEY DOING HERE?
WHAT THE HELL ARE THEY DOING ALIVE?
TRASH

USA= MUTANT FAG NATION
FAGS DOOMED
THANK GOD FOR ATOM
MUTANT FAGS ROT IN
REPENT MUTANT SCUM
GOD HATES MUTANT FAGS
GOD KILLED YOUR WORLD
GOD IS
MUTANT Lev.18:20 FAGS
GOD HATES MUTANT FAGS

MUTANTS, REANIMATED-AMERICANS, THREE-HEADED DOGS, EVEN CANNIBALS -- **NONE** HAD THE SHOCK VALUE OF SEEING THE **GOD HATES FAGS** LUNATICS. HERE, IN THE BOMBED-OUT SEAT OF OUR NASCENT SOCIETY, THE MONSTERS HAD ARRIVED.
WHERE'S A TRIBE OF RAVENOUS CANNIBALS WHEN YOU NEED ONE?
YEAH, IT'S AN ALL-YOU-CAN-EAT ASSHOLE BUFFET OVER THERE.
MAYBE THE CANNIBALS HAVE BETTER TASTE THAN THAT.
I UNDERSTAND ASSHOLE CAN BE QUITE CHEWY.
TRASH
GOD
THANK GOD
REPENT MUTANTS
GOD
FAGS
GOD
SPHINCTER QUIPS ASIDE, THIS ISN'T GOOD. I CAN'T REMEMBER IF THESE JERKS ARE VIOLENT OR NONVIOLENT.

BEING RAISED BY A SINGLE, WORKING MOM, FOR THE FIRST FEW YEARS OF MY SCHOOL LIFE I HAD A BABYSITTER; A KIND, CUBAN WOMAN NAMED CARMEN. SHE WAS A GOOD CATHOLIC AND HER TWO KIDS WENT TO PAROCHIAL SCHOOL, UNLIKE SECULAR ME, WHO ATTENDED PUBLIC SCHOOL. FROM A VERY EARLY AGE I KNEW RELIGION WAS HOKUM. WHAT I **DIDN'T** KNOW WAS TO KEEP STUFF LIKE THAT TO MYSELF.
I **HATE** YOU, JOSE! I **HATE** YOU! WHY DO YOU HAVE TO **RUIN** MY THINGS?
I DIDN'T RUIN NUTHIN'! YOUR "BOYFRIEND" LOOKS **BETTER** WITH A **MUSTACHE!**
I **HATE** YOU AND **GOD HATES YOU!** YOU'RE GONNA GO TO **HELL!**
I'M GONNA TELL **MAMA** YOU **CURSED ME!**
AND **I'M** GONNA TELL YOU **WRECKED** MY **TIGER BEAT** AN' YOU'RE GONNA HAVE TO BUY ME A **NEW ONE!**
"Hey, girl! Come Home With Me To Utah!"
WITHOUT THE MUSTACHE, DONNY OSMOND LOOKS LIKE A **GIRL**. I DID LUPE A **FAVOR**.
I DUNNO.
YEAH, **I DID!** ANYWAY, **GOD** WILL THINK IT'S FUNNY WHAT I DID.
I DON'T BELIEVE IN GOD.

YOU WHAT?
I DON'T BELIEVE IN GOD. I THINK IT'S SILLY, A MAN IN THE SKY WHO KNOWS EVERYTHING. IT'S DUMB.
YOU'RE DUMB!
OOF!
AND THUS ENDETH MY FIRST LESSON IN RELIGIOUS DIPLOMACY 101: "KEEPETH THY MOUTH SHUTTETH WHEN IT COMESETH TO GOD. ETH."
OH SHIT, HERE WE GO.
LET'S JUST LEAVE. I REALLY DON'T NEED A CONFRONTATION.
USA = MUTANT FAG TION
FAGS DOOMED THE WORLD
AS "NORMALS," WE ELECT YOU OUR MOUTHPIECES. HAVE AT 'EM!
HEY!

WHOA! DON'T BE GETTIN' NO FAG JUICE ON ME, Y'ALL.
WHATTAYA MEAN "FAG JUICE," BUDDY?
I AIN'T YER BUDDY, QUEER.
USA = MUTANT FAG
SEE THIS WOMAN? THIS IS MY WIFE. SHE HAS BREASTS AND A VAGINA.
DON'T BE GETTIN' ALL PORNY WITH ME, TINKERBELL. IN THEM TIGHT LEATHER PANTALOONS YOU AIN'T RUNNIN' FER HETERO OF THE MONTH.
TRASH
WIFE? WOMAN? BOOBS? PUNANI? BEEN TOGETHER FOR ALMOST TWENTY YEARS? ANY OF THAT PENETRATING?
NONE OF Y'ALL WILL BE PENETRATIN' ME, SODOMITE. SHE'S WHAT IS CALLED IN TH' LINGUA FAGGA, A "BEARD."
TRISH
THAT SOUP-STRAINER DANGLING FROM YOUR CHIN IS THE ONLY BEARD HERE.
TOUCHÉ.
"TOUCHÉ?" ISN'T THAT A TAD EFFETE, BUFORD?
TH' NAME'S ESTES.
ESTES. RHYMES WITH TESTES. GOT IT.

AN **OBSESSION** WITH TH' **MALE ORGANS.** MEBBE Y'ALL ARE ONE O' THEM ***TRANSSEXUAL HOMOSEXUALISTS.***
EVEN WITH ALL MY YEARS OF H.R. EXPERIENCE I'M AT A LOSS HOW TO DEAL WITH THIS HICK, OTHER THAN PUNCH HIM UPSIDE THE HEAD.
YOU'VE DONE A FINE JOB **BOTCHIN'** THIS COLLOQUY, ESTES. ***I'LL*** TAKE OVER.
SORRY, PASTOR FELCH.
AW, TESTES DROPPED THE BALL.
PUERILE PLAYS ON WORDS SPILL LIKE SO MUCH **VENOM** FROM A **SERPENT'S TONGUE, SODOMITE.**
TOUCHÉ!
I'D BE A LITTLE CONCERNED ABOUT ESTE'S FONDNESS FOR FRENCH.
OH, I'VE GOT MY EYE-BONES ON THAT'UN. **THA'S RIGHT, Y'ALL *HEARD* ME, ESTES.**
OKAY, SO LET'S START THIS PARLEY. **WHY** ARE YOU AGENTS OF INTOLERANCE HERE?

THESE ARE TH' END TIMES, LI'L MISSY, IN CASE Y'ALL HADN'T NOTICED. THE FAGS'VE BEEN INVITIN' TH' LORD'S WRATH FER AGES AN' FINALLY TIME COME FOR TH' ALMIGHTY T' SAY "ENOUGH IS ENOUGH!"
IS THAT SO?
INDEED IT IS. "TH' LORD WILL TAKE VENGEANCE ON HIS ADVERSARIES, AND HE RESERVETH WRATH FOR HIS ENEMIES."
CRASH
I GOTTA SAY, YOU SPEAKETH A BIT FLORIDLY.
SO EASY T' MOCK WHAT YA DON' UNNERSTAN', HEATHEN FAG. Y' MAY BURY YER MAN PARTS DEEP WITHIN YER GINGER CONCUBINE, BUT STILL Y'RE A FAG IN SERVICE OF BEELZEBUB.
ARE YOU TRYING TO TURN ME ON?
7
THIS'UN AND HIS CRIMSON-TRESSED INTIMATE ARE TH' WORST KINDA MUTATED SCUM! ON TH' SURFACE THESE TWO APPEAR UNCHANGED, BUT TH' WORM WORKS BEST IN PLEASIN' FORM!
FAG
FOR FOLKS WHO HATE ON GAYS THEY'RE SURE THEATRICAL.
IN THE PLUS COLUMN, HE DID SAY OUR FORMS ARE PLEASING.
7
CRASH

OKAY, ENOUGH'S ENOUGH! WHY'RE YOU BIBLE FREAKS HASSLING US? YOU'RE NOT FROM AROUND HERE!
INDEED NOT! WE'VE TRAVELED ALLA WAY FROM T'PEKA T'BEAR WITNESS T' TH' FINAL MOMENTS O' FAGDOM'S REIGN ON EARTH BEFORE WE GIT SWEPT UP T' TH' LORD'S BOSOM.
YOU THINK THIS IS BOOK OF REVELATIONS-TYPE GOINGS ON? I WAS RAISED RELIGIOUS AND I KNOW THE JIBBAJABBA SAINT JOHN LAID OUT. MONSTERS LIKE A LION, CALF, EAGLE AND ONE WITH A FACE OF A DUDE.
"AN' TH' FOUR BEASTS HAD EACH OF 'EM SIX WINGS ABOUT HIM; AND THEY WERE FULLA EYES WITHIN: AND THEY REST NOT DAY AN' NIGHT, SAYIN', HOLY, HOLY, HOLY, LORD GOD ALMIGHTY, WHICH WAS, AND IS, AND IS T' COME."
YEAH, YEAH. AND BUGS WITH CROWNS.
"AN' TH' SHAPES O' TH' LOCUSTS WERE LIKE UNTO HORSES PREPARED UNTO BATTLE; AN' ON THEIR HEADS WERE AS IT WERE CROWNS LIKE GOLD, AND THEIR FACES WERE AS TH' FACES O' MEN."
YEAH. SO, BUGS WITH PEOPLE FACES. THAT'S SOME CRAZY SHIT.
GET A GOOD LOOK IN TH' MIRROR LATELY, SON?
OKAY, I'M OUT.
POINT, RELIGIOUS LOONY.
TRASH

SLUT. JEZEBEL.
HUSSY. VIXEN.
WHAT'S IT LIKE TO HAVE NEVER HAD AN ORGASM?
AS YOU MISBEGOTTEN OFF-SPRING OF **GOG** AND **MAGOG** SCRAPE AND SCURRY IN TH' RUBBLE, D'YA EVEN CONTEMPLATE HOW IT ALL COME T' THIS?
SIT YE DOWN AN' I'LL EDUCATE, **FAGS** AND **FAGGETTES. TSUNAMIS** AND **KATRINAS** AN' **9/11s** WERE ALL WELL 'N' GOOD, BUT TH' PLANET WAS STILL FESTERIN' WITH **SIN** AND **FAGGOTRY**.
DO WE **HAVE** TO LISTEN TO THIS?
COLOR ME MASOCHISTIC, BUT I'M FASCINATED.
GOD HATES FAGS
GOD
GOD'S **BIG BLUE MARBLE** HAD TURNED INTA A **SWIRLIN' JIZZBALL OF HOMOSEXUALITY**. AN' WE BESEECHED TH' LORD OVER AN' OVER: **SMITE** THESE **FAGGOTS** AN' **BE DONE WITH IT**. WE THANKED GOD FOR HIS CLEANSIN' GIFT OF **AIDS**. BUT IT WERE SLOW AS MOLASSES AN' WEREN'T ENOUGH.
YOU POOR BABIES.
BUT, THROUGH **PERSEVERANCE, PROTESTIN'** AN' **PRAYER**, WE FINALLY GOT GOD T' GIFT THIS FALLEN WORLD WITH HIS GLORIOUS **NUKES** AN' **CHEMICAL WEAPONS. PRAISE BE!**
RIIIIGHT. BECAUSE **GOD** KEEPS AN ARSENAL OF **MAN-MADE WEAPONS** AT **HIS** DISPOSAL.
GOD

AND ONCE AGAIN, YOU'RE HERE WHY?
WE'RE HERE IN WHAT'S LEFT O' NEW SODOM T' PROTEST TH' LAST OF YOUR FILTHY KIND. AN' WHEN OUR WORK IS DONE WE'LL--
OKAY, THAT'S IT. I'M BORED. YOU'RE BORING. C'MON, SWEETIE, LET'S GO.
TRASH
SO, WE GOT BACK TO THE BUSINESS OF LIVING. AFTER A WHILE, FELCH AND HIS RADIATION-SICK FLOCK FADED INTO THE BACKGROUND, THEIR ROTE PROTESTING MUTED TO TRIFLING WHITE NOISE.
ARE CARROTS SUPPOSED TO LOOK LIKE THIS?
IT'S JUST HAPPY TO SEE YOU.
FAGS!
THIS LITTLE HUT'S LOOKING PRETTY SWANK.
YEAH, IT'S NOT TOO BAD FOR A DUMP.
I CAN'T WAIT TO DECORATE.
FAGS!
7

IT DIDN'T MATTER THE ACTIVITY -- DAY OR NIGHT, NIGHT OR DAY -- THERE THEY WERE, PICKETING AND HARANGUING US, WITHOUT STOP.
FAGS!
DID HE JUST CALL US FAGS WHILE WE'RE HAVING SEX?
GOTTA ADMIRE THEIR COMMITMENT.
I WAS NEVER BIG ON EGGPLANT, BUT MUTANT EGGPLANT? NOT BAD.
THAT A CRACK AT MY EXPENSE, CRACKER? HA HA HA.
OH, YOU.
FAGS! ≥COUGH-COUGH≤
HEY, PHRED, THAT COUGH SOUNDS PRETTY BAD. YOU WANT SOMETHING TO EAT?
EVEN YER CARROTS'RE CORRUPTED BY TH' SOIL FROM WHENCE -- ≥COUGH-COUGH≤ -- THEY GROW!
SUIT YOURSELF.
FAGS!
EVEN WITH THE FILTER OF FAMILIARITY DULLING FELCH & CO.'S ONSLAUGHT, ON OCCASION MICHELE AND I NEEDED A BREAK AND WOULD GO OFF TO VISIT UNDEAD ED, MARY AND CAESAR...

IT'S GOOD TO BE AWAY FROM THE MUTANT CAMP.
THOSE CLOWNS WITH THE SIGNS STILL MALINGERING, HUH?
YEAH, THEY DON'T QUIT.
YOUR HOUSE CAN'T BE **THAT** NICE. LEAVE.
IT **ISN'T**, BUT WE DON'T WANT TO ABANDON OUR FRIENDS. FUNNY THE PROTESTORS DON'T COME HERE.
SEEING REANIMATED CORPSES PUTS A BIG QUESTION MARK ON THEIR NOTION OF AN AFTERLIFE. IT'S WHY THEY HATE ATHEISTS: IF YOU MAKE 'EM DOUBT -- *EVEN* FOR A SECOND -- THAT'S ONE SECOND TOO MANY.
VIGGO WAS **SO** THE **HOTNESS**. I HOPE **HE** DIDN'T GET PERISHED.
AGREED.
HE'D HAVE DIED YOUNG AND LEFT A GOOD-LOOKING CORPSE, THO'. MAYBE HE'D BE UNDEAD LIKE ME. NOT THAT I'M GOOD-LOOKING ANY MORE.
YOU LOOK FINE.
GLAM WEEKLY
YOU ARE **SUCH** THE **LIAR**.
LOTS OF **MODELS** WOULD'VE **KILLED** FOR YOUR FIGURE.
THAT'S TRUE.

SO, YOU DIDN'T BELIEVE IN AN AFTER-LIFE?
RELIGION'S BUNKUM. REANIMATION ISN'T SOME SUPERNATURAL METAPHYSICAL MUMBO-JUMBO. BEFORE THE APOCALYPSE WE MOSTLY DIDN'T EVEN KNOW WHAT WE DIDN'T KNOW, LET ALONE KNOW WHAT WE KNEW. IF WE COULD FIND A SCIENTIST OR DOCTOR, MAYBE HE COULD EXPLAIN IT. BUT SURE AS SHIT A CLERGYMAN COULDN'T.
YOU'RE MY KINDA REANIMATED CORPSE, ED.
UGGGGGH! WHEN THE PINK THING COMES OUT, NO MORE BELLY-RUBBING FOR POOCHIE. AND THREE PINK THINGS? YUCK.
WHO'S A BAD DOG? YOU ARE, CAESAR, YOU ARE. HEH HEH
EXCEPT FOR THE FLIES AND THE SMELL, I REALLY LIKE THEM. IT'S A SHAME THEY AND THE MUTANTS DON'T COZY UP.
AH, THEY'LL COME AROUND.
I WISH THOSE PROTESTORS WOULD LEAVE. MAYBE WE SHOULD BUG OUT.
"BUG OUT"? WHAT IS THIS, M.A.S.H.?

YOU KNOW WHAT I MEAN. THEY'RE BUMMING ME OUT.
ME TOO. I HAVE NO TROUBLE HATING, BUT SEEING ALL THEIR HATE KIND OF MAKES ME LOSE MY ZEST FOR IT. IT LOOKS SO UGLY.
MAYBE THAT'S THEIR SECRET: THEY LEECH AWAY THEIR PREY'S VIGOR FOR HATE.
IT'S CRIMINAL: THEY'VE TAKEN ALL THE FUN OUT OF HATE.
DID WE JUST DO A PUBLIC SERVICE COMMERCIAL?
HEY, CHICAS, WHAT'S UP?
AH, WE'RE FUCKIN' PERTURBED. NO DISRESPECT FOR MY HONEYBUNS, HERE, BUT WITH HER DISTENDED GRILLE WE CAN'T EXACTLY KISS ANY MORE.
YEAH, IT'S REALLY EATING HER.
EATING? DON'T GET ME STARTED ON THAT!

I DIDN'T REALIZE YOU TWO WERE, UH, LESBI--
WHAT'RE YOU, HALF-RETARDED?
I GUESS. BOY, YOU GUYS MUST REALLY HATE THOSE GOD HATES FAGS CREEPS.
Y'NOTICE HOW SICKLY THOSE MOTHERFUCKERS ARE? THEY AIN'T GONNA BE AROUND LONG. WHY WASTE THE ENERGY?
GUYS, GUYS! TROUBLE!
AGAIN?
SEE? NEW JESUS NUTS...
...TRYING TO TAKE CREDIT FOR THE GLORIOUS END OF DAYS WE ALL BEAR WITNESS TO?
DON' END YER SENTENCES ON A PREPOSITION, FOOL! OUR GOOD WORKS DID BRING ABOUT THIS RIGHTEOUS APOCALYPSE.
I'M A WRITER AND I'LL END MY SENTENCES HOW I PLEASE. THIS APOCALYPSE IS INDEED RIGHTEOUS, BUT PRAYER ALONE DIDN'T BRING IT.
FAG
GOD

EXCUSE ME, BUT WHO THE EFF ARE YOU AND WHAT THE EFF ARE YOU EFFING A-HOLES TALKING ABOUT?
PASTOR JERROTHY J. LAHAYGEE. AND I DON'T APPRECIATE THAT KIND OF ALMOST POTTY TALK, MISSY. ANYWAY, IT WASN'T FELCH AND HIS SIGN-TOTING TOADIES THAT GAVE US THIS SPLENDID HOLOCAUST-- FORGIVE MY CHOICE OF WORD IF YOU'RE JEWISH.
NO PROBLEMO.
THE JEWS REJECTED GOD AND HIS WAYS. LET THEM BURN.
JESUS DID NOT COME TO EARTH TO BE THE MESSIAH, SO HOW COULD THE JEWS REJECT WHAT WAS NEVER OFFERED?
POPPYCOCK, ZIONIST SWINE!
OH HUSH. PLENTY OF GOOD CHRISTIANS IN SEARCH OF ESCHATOLOGICAL LITERATURE SNAPPED UP MY LEFT ALONE SERIES. BUT GRIPPING EPICS WEREN'T ENOUGH.
YOU'RE THE GUY WHO WROTE THOSE THINGS? YEESH. OKAY, GO ON.
AHEM UNLIKE SOME PENNY ANTE PASTORS, MY MEGACHURCH BROUGHT IN A LOTTA GREEN.
LEFT ALONE
I SENT MY MOST APPLE-CHEEKED PARISHIONERS TO FORMER SOVIET REPUBLICS TO BUY LOOSE NUKES AND COMPONENTS. ONLY ONCE DID ONE OF OUR BLUE-HAIRED BUYERS GET PULLED FOR A RANDOM SECURITY CHECK AND SHE EXPLAINED THE DEVICE AWAY AS A MEDICINE PUMP.
MOSTLY THEY CHOSE SWARTHY FOLKS WHO NEED A SHAVE. SON, I BET YOU GOT PULLED OFF LINES ALLA TIME. GET IT? ALLAH TIME? ALLAH. NEVER MIND.
THE APOCALYPSE IS ONE THING, BUT BAD PUNNING?

WE EVEN KIDNAPPED TOM CRUISE AND OVERNIGHTED HIM TO BEN GURION INTERNATIONAL STRAPPED TO A HUNDRED CASES OF RED BULL.
OKAY, I'LL BITE: UM, WHY?
YOU NEED A FLAWLESS RED HEIFER IN THE HOLY LAND TO BRING ABOUT ARMAGEDDON. HADDA IMPROVISE.
AND...?
THE ANTICHRIST HAS TO BE IN ISRAEL TO BRING ON ARMAGEDDON. TOM CRUISE IS THE ANTICHRIST. DID YOU SEE HIM JUMPING UP AND DOWN ON OPRAH'S COUCH? CHILLING.
UH-HUH. AND...?
THE PROPHET DANIEL WROTE THAT THE ANTICHRIST "DOES NOT REGARD THE DESIRE OF WOMEN." HELLO? TOM CRUISE? WITH THE BEARD?
A BEARD! JUS' LIKE THIS FELLER AN' HIS RUSSET-TRESSED CONCUBINE!
OH, SHUT UP, YOU!
MUTANT
WE CALLED THE F.B.I. SAYING WE KNEW OF AN IRANIAN PLAN TO SIMULTANEOUSLY EXPLODE NUCLEAR SUITCASE BOMBS IN SEVEN AMERICAN CITIES. AN AMERICAN HIROSHIMA.
NUKING HUMANKIND IS HOW YOU CHOSE TO MAKE GOD HAPPY? UNBELIEVABLE.
WE SAT BACK AND WATCHED THE TRAILS ACROSS THE SKY AS UNCLE SAM DID THE REST. THAT'S HOW YA GET GOD TO SIT UP AND TAKE NOTICE.

ATTENTION! ATTENTION!
NOW WHAT?
YAY! MORE INTERLOPERS. IF I'D HAVE KNOWN THE APOCALYPSE WAS GOING TO BE THIS STRESSFUL I'D HAVE NEVER--
PLEASE DESIST FROM ISSUING THE REST OF THAT BON MOT, CITIZEN.
WELL, THAT GOT MY ATTENTION.
THANK YOU, SIR. LADIES, GENTLEMEN, MUTANTS AND OTHERS, WE REQUEST THAT YOU FOLLOW THESE INSTRUCTIONS: HEALTHY HUMANS AND MUTANTS COME WITH US! EVERYONE ELSE, PLEASE ACCOMPANY MY SQUAD-MATES FOR, UH, "MEDICAL TREATMENT."

BEFORE YOU EVEN ASK, SIRS, **YOU** AND YOUR **SORE-COVERED CONFEDERATES** ARE **"EVERYONE ELSE."** GO WITH SQUAD 2.
GOD HATES
SO, DO WE GO WITH THEM?
WHO ARE WE TO DISTRUST ANONYMOUS, WELL-ARMED REPRESENTATIVES OF ORIGIN AND INTENT UNKNOWN?
A TRULY CUTTING BON MOT, CITIZEN.
HOW CAN I **NOT** LOVE THIS GUY?

ATTENTION DELUSIONAL ZEALOTS WHO HAD NOTHING TO DO WITH CAUSING ANY OF THIS -- REALLY, THOSE RUSKIES SOLD YOU GULLIBLE SAPS THE ARMS EQUIVALENTS OF PLACEBOS -- PLEASE POSE BY THE GIANT OPEN GRAVE-LIKE HOLE IN THE GROUND FOR A NICE, UM, COMMEMORATIVE PICTURE.
HEY, WHAT'S WITH TH' GUNS?
UH, NOT GUNS, SIR. THESE ARE SPECIAL LONG-LENSED DIGITAL CAMERAS. JUST SMILE AND SAY, "JESUS."
7

WELL, WHATEVER WAS AILING THEM, I'M BETTING THEY'RE CURED NOW.
RATATATATATAT!
YOUR WIT IS YOUR UMBRELLA, CITIZEN. PLEASE FOLLOW ME. AND BY THE WAY, CITIZEN: NICE PANTS.
OH FOR THE LOVE OF...
ANYONE ELSE HERE NERVOUS ABOUT THIS LATEST DEVELOPMENT?
OUR CHAPERONES ARE A TAD UN-NERVING, YES.
NOT TO MENTION THE SOUND OF GUNFIRE ECHOING THROUGH THE AIR.
YEAH, BUT I WON'T MOURN THOSE SANCTIMONIOUS PRICKS.
HEY, HAZMAT GUY, WHERE ARE WE GOING AND ARE YOU PLANNING ON "MEDICALLY TREAT-ING" US, TOO?
YOUR SARCASM IS RAPIER SHARP, CITIZEN. NO, WE JUST WANT YOU TO ACCOMPANY US TO MIDTOWN FOR A GATHERING.
WHAT? LIKE BURNING MAN?
VERY WITTY. YOU AND YOUR SIG-NIFICANT OTHER ARE WELL-PAIRED, MA'AM.
YOU GET "CITIZEN," I GET "MA'AM." IS HE TRYING TO MAKE ME FEEL OLD?
HOW COULD MY CHILD BRIDE BE OLD?

HEY, HAZMAT GUY, HOW FAR ARE WE GOING?
MIDTOWN. 48TH AND SIXTH AVENUE.
ON FOOT?
E.M.P. WIPED OUT ALL TRANSPORTATION. IT'S GOOD EXERCISE.
MISFIT
I'M WEARING SIXTY POUNDS OF APPARATUS AND YOU DON'T HEAR ME COMPLAINING, CITIZEN.
WE GOT JACK LaLANNE LEADING US WHO KNOWS WHERE.
48TH AND SIXTH IS RIGHT NEAR WHERE MY OFFICE WAS.
HEY, HAZMAT GUY, YOU TRYING TO GIVE MY WIFE FLASHBACKS TO THE BAD OLD DAYS?
YOU'RE A FUNNY FELLOW, CITIZEN. I'M SURE YOU AND YOUR SPOUSE WILL BE VERY POPULAR.
WITH WHO?

AFTER TREKKING FOR WHAT FELT LIKE MANY HOURS, BUT MIGHT ONLY HAVE BEEN SEVERAL HOURS, WE ARRIVED AT THE SKELETAL REMAINS OF AN OFFICE BUILDING.
News Corporation
News
HOLY SHIT, THIS PLACE IS PACKED.
THIS IS WHERE **POX NEWS** WAS.
GOOD RIDDANCE.
THE SIZE OF THE CROWD SURPRISED US. MOST LOOKED AS HEALTHY AS MICHELE AND I. A HUSHED, EXPECTANT MURMUR FLOATED ABOVE THE CROWD.
PLEASE JOIN THE OTHER CITIZENS, CITIZENS.
SUCH MANNERS. IF **EMILY POST** AND **DARTH VADER** HAD A BABY...

SPEAKING OF ALL THINGS STAR WARS, "I'VE GOT A BAD FEELING ABOUT THIS."
BECAUSE THIS SITUATION IS SO UNSETTLING I'LL FORGIVE THAT LAPSE INTO HEINOUS DORKDOM.
IS THAT... IS THAT A BLIMP?
IS THAT--?
OH NO. IT CAN'T BE...

EVENING, CONGREGANTS. GLAD YOU COULD ALL MAKE IT TO THE FIRST EVER ASSEMBLY OF ***THE COUNCIL OF MODOZ.***
I AM ***MODOZ.*** WELCOME!
NOOOOOOOO!
LIKE A FUCKED-UP PHOENIX RISING FROM THE ASHES, PUTRID PUNDIT AND BANE OF MY TELEVIEWING EXISTENCE, **RILE O'BILEY**, FLOATED ABOVE THE ANXIOUS ASSEMBLY, HIS TRADEMARK SUPERCILIOUS SMIRK REPLACED BY A BENIGN, ODDLY BEATIFIED SMILE. THE APOCALYPSE I COULD DEAL WITH, BUT ***THIS?***

NO.
NO. NOT O'BILEY.
FOR FUCK'S SAKES...
SINCE MY LATE TEENS I'VE BEEN A LATE-NIGHTER, HITTING THE SACK AROUND DAWN AND RISING IN EARLY AFTERNOON.
FOR YEARS, DUE TO A HEART CONDITION, I COULDN'T HAVE CAFFEINE, EVEN THOUGH I LIKED COFFEE. EVENTUALLY I GOT THE CONDITION TAKEN CARE OF, BUT I STILL AVOIDED CAFFEINE. AND THIS IS RELEVANT HOW?

BECAUSE MY WAKER-UPPER INSTEAD WAS A BRACING DOSE OF CURRENT EVENTS. I'D START LIGHT, WITH DULL, PREDICTABLE MAINSTREAM CNN, THEN HIT THE USUAL "LEFTIE" SITES LIKE THE HUFFINGTON POST AND CROOKS AND LIARS TO PERK UP MY BLOOD. AS A COUNTERPOINT I'D SWITCH OVER TO THE POX NEWS SITE AND NO ONE -- NO ONE -- COULD ROUSE ME FROM MY TORPOR LIKE THEIR RESIDENT DEMAGOGUE, RILE O'BILEY. HIS ERRATIC COMBO OF SNAKE OIL CHARM AND BELLICOSE SCHOOLYARD BULLYING WAS DARK ART.
...VILE TO ALLOW SUCH HATE SPEECH ON THAT WEBSITE...
RILE O'BILEY
OH, RILE, REALLY. YOU HAVE EVEN WORSE COMMENTS ON YOUR WEBSI--
NO! THAT'S A LIE! SHUT UP! SHUT! UP! HUFFINGTON IS WORSE THAN THE K.K.K. AND THE NAZIS COMBINED TIMES INFINITY-BILLION!
RILE, THAT'S ABSUR--
SHUT UP. CUT HIS MIC! I WON'T HAVE PINHEADS WHO CONDONE HATE ON MY SHOW! PEOPLE WHO HATE SHOULD BE BEATEN TO DEATH AND FED TO RABID WOLVERINES. SHE PUTS UP ALL THAT VILE STUFF. I MEAN, IT'S A SEWER.
POX NEWS
THE O'BILEY
SHE KEEPS HER LITTLE MANICURED NAILS CLEAN? NO! IT'S HER! IT'S HUFFINGTON! IT'S HER! NO LOOFAH MITT IN THE WORLD COULD GET HER CLEAN, NO MATTER HOW MUCH ATTENTION IT PAID TO EVERY SENSUOUS CREVICE ON HER-- AHEM SHE'S A FOXY, EXOTIC, HORRIBLE, EVIL WITCH. A HOT, SEXY NAZI, LIKE ILSA, SHE-WOLF OF THE SS!
RE-MARK-A-BLE.
THIS HAS SO GOT TO SUCK FOR YOU.
I'M SPEECHLESS.

HI, I'M MODOZ. THANKS FOR WATCHING US TONIGHT. "ARE THERE ANY REMAINING QUESTIONS?" THAT IS THE SUBJECT OF TONIGHT'S TALKING POINTS MEM-- ER, UH -- INAUGURAL COUNCIL OF MODOZ CONVERGENCE.
I AM RISEN, RECHRISTENED MODOZ AND I BRING TO THE CHOSEN A MESSAGE OF HOPE (AND BEFORE YOU GET ALL WORRIED, I'M NOT JUST TALKING ABOUT THE JEWS).
EARLIER THIS YEAR I WARNED THAT THE WORLD MIGHT END. I MIGHT NOT HAVE PUT IT IN THOSE EXACT WORDS, BUT I INTIMATED THAT IF THINGS KEPT GOING THE WAY THEY WERE, BANGO! AND HERE WE ARE.
HE'S TAKING CREDIT FOR BEING A PROPHET OF DOOM?
LOOKS LIKE.
WHAT'S UP WITH THAT BIG ASS HEAD? HE HAD A BIG HEAD BEFORE ALL THIS, BUT DAMN.
I'M IN NO POSITION TO JUDGE ODD SWELLINGS.
POINT TAKEN.

COME AND GATHER YOURSELVES TOGETHER UNTO THE SUPPER OF THE GREAT MODOZ; THAT YE MAY EAT THE FLESH OF KINGS, AND THE FLESH OF CAPTAINS, AND THE FLESH OF MIGHTY MEN, AND THE FLESH OF HORSES, AND OF THEM THAT SIT ON THEM, AND THE FLESH OF ALL MEN, BOTH FREE AND BOND, BOTH SMALL AND GREAT.
ARE YOU ADVOCATING CANNIBALISM? BEEN THERE, DONE THAT!
NO, THAT'S WRONG. THERE'S FOOD AND DRINK HERE FOR THE CHOSEN, THAT'S ALL. AND SHELTER.
REVELATION 19. ANOTHER A-HOLE QUOTING SCRIPTURE. I'M GONNA FLIP!
"MODOZ" IS GETTING ALL RELIGIOUSY ON US.
I SEE A LOT OF WORRIED FACES OUT THERE. AND DIRTY. VERY DIRTY. INSIDE THE BUNKER ARE SHOWERS AND LOOFAHS FOR ALL WHO ARE WORTHY. AND WHAT MAKES ONE WORTHY? ONLY THAT YOU'RE A GOOD AMERICAN OF FIT BREEDING STOCK.
YES, FOLKS, IF AMERICA IS TO REGAIN ITS FORMER GLORY, WE NEED TO START MAKING GOOD, HEALTHY, BABIES, SO SAY I, THE GREAT AND POWERFUL MODOZ!
THIS IS RIDICULOUS. I GET IT: PICK A "TRUSTED" FACE FROM TV, MAKE HIM SPOKES-CYBORG FOR THE NEW RELIGION.
I CAN'T STOP MYSELF. I'M GONNA HECKLE.
TESTIFY, BR'ER BOB.

HAVEN'T ANY OF YOU SEEN THE WIZARD OF OZ?
I LOVE THAT MOVIE!
YEAH, ME TOO. SHUT UP, SPOIL-SPORT!
HE IS RISEN, LIKE HE SAID. WE CAN'T FLY! HE'S HOLY!
IT MAKES SENSE!
YEAH, SHUT UP! I AM THE GREAT AND POWERFUL MODOZ!
OKAY, WAIT. NOT JUST THE WIZARD OF OZ. MARVEL COMICS. HE'S TOTALLY RIPPING OFF MODOK, THE MENTAL ORGANISM DESIGNED ONLY FOR KILLING!
LOOKS LIKE WE HAVE A NERD HERE TODAY, FOLKS. LOOK AT THIS WORLD. IT'S THE NERDS THAT DID THIS TO US. SCIENCE MADE THIS WORLD A SMOKING RUIN.
I, ON THE OTHER HAND, HAVE A FAIR AND BALANCED PROPOSAL: COME IN AND LIVE COMFORTABLY AND IN RETURN MAKE NEW AMERICAN BABIES. THAT, MY FRIENDS, IS A WIN/WIN DEAL!
WHAT'S GOTTA HAPPEN TO YOU IDIOTS? DOES A BOMB HAVE TO DROP ON YOUR HEADS TO MAKE YOU STOP BELIEVING THIS CRAP? OH WAIT.
YET HERE WE ARE, LISTENING TO SOME FALSE PROPHET. THIS ISN'T THE MIDDLE AGES. THIS ISN'T THE DAWN OF MAN.
SHUT UP! SHUT IT! IT IS THE DAWN OF MAN! THE NEW DAWN OF MAN!

IT WAS A BRAVE EFFORT, SWEETIE, BUT THE CROWD SMELLS CLEAN LINENS IN ITS FUTURE. EVEN I HAVE TO ADMIT THAT SOUNDS PRETTY GOOD.
ET TU? ⋛SIGH⋚ I KNOW WHAT YOU MEAN, BUT **NO.**
I UNDERSTAND. WE CAN BUILD AN ADDITION ONTO OUR HOVEL.
I THOUGHT YOU **LIKED** THE SHACK.
ALL OF A SUDDEN YOU'RE **GRIZZLY ADAMS**? YOU **HATE** ROUGHING IT.
LOOK WHERE WE ARE: ***POX NEWS HQ.*** IT'S SHELTER IN THE **BELLY OF THE BEAST!**
SHUT UP! PEOPLE ARE HERE TO HEAR **ME, NOT YOU, PINHEAD!** I AM **MODOZ! HEED ME!**
THE **PENIS** IS **GOOD**. THE **PENIS** SHOOTS **SEEDS** AND MAKES **NEW LIFE**, AND **GIFTS** THE EARTH WITH A **BLESSING OF MEN**, AS ONCE IT WAS.
HE'S MAKING SISSY ON ONE OF MY TOUCHSTONES.
YOU WANNA HOODWINK A BUNCH OF MALNOURISHED RUBES? ***FINE!*** BUT **STOP** MISQUOTING ***ZARDOZ!***
THE SPEECH GOES: "THE **PENIS** IS ***EVIL***. THE **PENIS** SHOOTS **SEEDS**, AND MAKES **NEW LIFE**, AND ***POISONS*** THE EARTH WITH A ***PLAGUE OF MEN***, AS ONCE IT WAS!"
CUT HIS MIC! GET THIS UPPITY NERD OUT OF HERE!

NOT EVERYONE APPRECIATES JAPES AND BARBS, CITIZEN. IF YOU'D COME WITH ME. YOU CAN STAY, MA'AM.
ARE YOU HIGH? EVEN THOUGH YOU KEEP CALLING ME **"MA'AM,"** WHICH I DON'T APPRECIATE, I'M NOT **ABAN-DONING** MY HUSBAND FOR THREE HOTS AND A COT.
THANKS, SWEETIE.
YOU HAVE YOURSELF A REAL SPECIAL LADY, CITIZEN.
DON'T I KNOW IT.
YOU BETTER GODDAMN WELL KNOW IT. BACK TO THE STUPID, RUSTY, DUSTY HUT.
ACCOMMODATIONS BELOW ARE A **LOT** NICER THAN **COTS** AND **M.R.E.s.**
≶SIGH≷ MR. BIG-MOUTH FUCKS UP AGAIN.
IT'S OKAY. I DON'T BLAME YOU FOR MOUTHING OFF AT YOUR MOST HATED FACE FROM TV.
REALLY?
NO. I BLAME YOU. BUT I'LL GET OVER IT. ANYWAY, HOW WOULD YOU LIKE YOUR SCABBY MUTANT RAT PREPARED TONIGHT?
≶DOUBLE SIGH≷

SEEMS KIND OF LONELY HERE WITHOUT BYRON, CINDY AND LENORE.
MM-HMM.
YOU'RE REALLY MAD AT ME, AREN'T YOU?
MM-HMM.
BUT... BUT YOU SAID YOU UNDERSTOOD.
MM-HMM.
UH, NO OFFENSE, BUT WE'LL LEAVE YOU TWO TO YOUR DOMESTIC "SITUATION."
AND THEN THERE WERE TWO.
MAYBE MR. BIGMOUTH SHOULD GIVE SAID ORIFICE A REST.
MM-HMM. **NOW** YOU'RE LEARNING.

G'NIGHT, SWEETIE. I LOVE YOU.
MM-HMM.
HEY, WE DON'T GO TO BED MAD, REMEMBER?
MM-HMM.
BUT...
I'LL BE OVER IT TOMORROW, BOB. NOW LET ME SLEEP ON OUR NIT-INFESTED PILE OF FILTHY RAGS.

I WAS NEVER A FAN OF WHAT I CALL "COUNTRY DARK." ONE OF THE MAIN REASONS I LIKED CITY LIVING WAS IT WAS NEVER REALLY ALL THE WAY DARK. BUT NOW THINGS WERE DIFFERENT AND COUNTRY DARK REIGNED SUPREME.

OVER THE COURSE OF THAT CHILLY NIGHT -- EVEN THOUGH IT WAS QUITE WARM TEMPERATURE-WISE, IF YOU CATCH MY DRIFT -- WE FOUND OURSELVES HOISTED FROM OUR BEDDING, HOODED, AND BORNE ACROSS THE WASTELANDS ON THE BACKS OF SHADOWY FIGURES.
BOB! WHAT'S HAPPENING?
I DUNNO, SWEETIE! HEY! PUT US DOWN! THIS ISN'T FUNNY!

WHO ARE YOU? WHERE ARE YOU TAKING US?
OH CHRIST, I HOPE IT ISN'T THOSE FUCKING CANNIBALS!
NO MATTER HOW MANY TIMES WE ASKED -- IN VOICES STRAINED BY CONFUSION AND FEAR -- WHO OUR CAPTORS WERE AND WHERE THEY WERE TAKING US, NO ANSWERS CAME UNTIL...

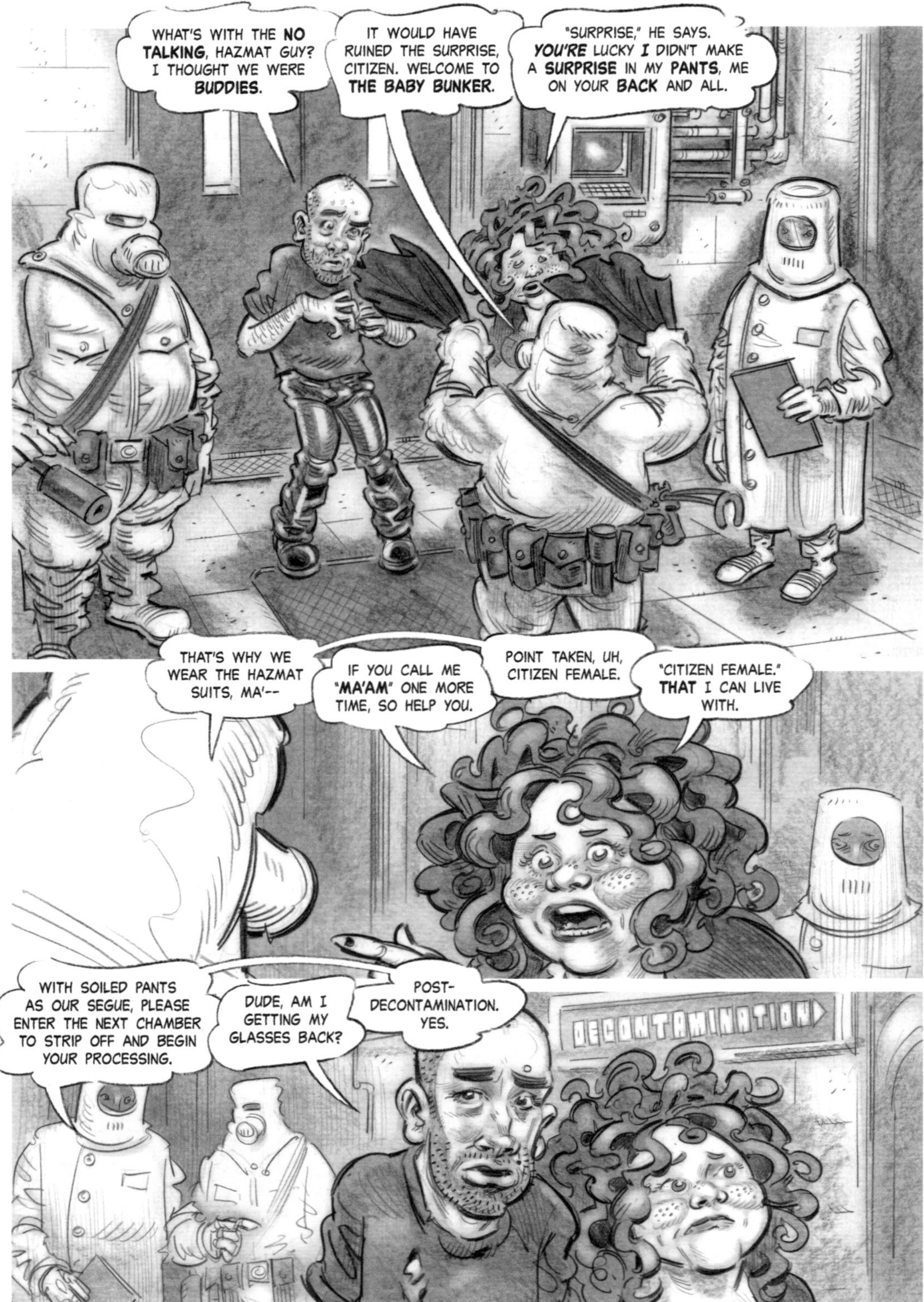
WHAT'S WITH THE **NO TALKING**, HAZMAT GUY? I THOUGHT WE WERE **BUDDIES**.
IT WOULD HAVE RUINED THE SURPRISE, CITIZEN. WELCOME TO **THE BABY BUNKER**.
"SURPRISE," HE SAYS. ***YOU'RE*** LUCKY ***I*** DIDN'T MAKE A **SURPRISE** IN MY **PANTS**, ME ON YOUR **BACK** AND ALL.
THAT'S WHY WE WEAR THE HAZMAT SUITS, MA'--
IF YOU CALL ME "**MA'AM**" ONE MORE TIME, SO HELP *YOU*.
POINT TAKEN, UH, CITIZEN FEMALE.
"CITIZEN FEMALE." **THAT** I CAN LIVE WITH.
WITH SOILED PANTS AS OUR SEGUE, PLEASE ENTER THE NEXT CHAMBER TO STRIP OFF AND BEGIN YOUR PROCESSING.
DUDE, AM I GETTING MY GLASSES BACK?
POST-DECONTAMINATION. YES.
DECONTAMINATION

THIS IS A BIT DEHUMANIZING.
AH, IT'S NOT SO BAD.
YOU USED TO PITCH A FIT IN A **PRIVATE CHANGING BOOTH!** ALL OF A SUDDEN YOU'RE **JOE NUDIST?**
IT'S THE END OF THE WORLD AND I FEEL FINE.
PLEASE PLACE CLOTHES IN BIN
YOU DON'T EVEN **LIKE** R.E.M.! ***WHO ARE YOU?***
GO WITH THE FLOW, BABY.
I WANT MY HUSBAND BACK.
(I HAVE TO KEEP TALKING TO PREVENT A WORRY-BONER. WORK WITH ME.)
THAT'S MY HUSBAND.
HEY, DO WE GET OUR CLOTHES BACK AFTER THEY'RE CLEANED?
IF BY **CLEANED** YOU MEAN **DESTROYED, NO.**
WAIT, **WHAT? *DESTROYED?*** B-BUT THOSE ARE QUALITY LEATHER PANTS.

I THOUGHT YOU HATED THOSE.
I DID. I DO. BUT THEY'RE FINALLY BROKEN IN. THEY'RE COMFORTABLE AND STURDY. MAD MAX, REMEMBER?
I TELL YOU WHAT, SIR, WE'LL STOW THEM FOR YOU SO YOU CAN GET A WHIFF ONCE YOU'RE CLEANED UP.
HEY, I BATHE EVERY FEW DAYS.
WHEN YOU GET YOUR SENSE OF SMELL BACK WE'LL TALK.
YOU HAVE LOVELY HAIR.
THANK YOU.
YES. IT'S MADE A FINE HOME TO MANY EXOTIC INSECTS.
Y-YOU'RE NOT GOING TO HAVE TO SHAVE MY HEAD ARE YOU?
NO. JUST SUBJECT IT TO A MILDLY SCALP-SINGEING SHAMPOO PROCESS.

WHEN'S THE LAST TIME YOU BUZZED YOUR HAIR, SIR?
JEEZ, I DUNNO. SINCE BEFORE ALL THIS. I DIDN'T REALLY THINK ABOUT IT, BUT IT SORT OF STOPPED GROWING OUT. WEIRD.
INDEED.
AS GITMO/AUSCHWITZ/SING SING AS THIS ALL IS, I'M LOOKING FORWARD TO A **REAL** SHOWER.
MY **SCALP** FEELS LIKE IT'S ON **FIRE**. ***I'D LIKE TO RINSE, PLEASE!***
WHOO! NOW **THAT'S** WATER PRESSURE! IF THIS WASN'T ALL SO CLINICAL IT WOULD BE EXHILARATING.
IF IT POWER-STRIPS THE BUG-GOO OUT OF MY HAIR I'LL BE ***THRILLED***.
UH, **HELLO?** NOW WHAT? YOU DESTROYED OUR CLOTHES.
YOU'LL BE GIVEN NEW WARDROBE AFTER YOU TOWEL OFF.
OOH, NEW CLOTHES!

I DON'T MEAN TO KVETCH, BUT AREN'T WE A LITTLE **OLD** FOR FOOTIE PAJAMAS?
I'VE BEEN WARNED ABOUT YOUR SMART MOUTH, FINGERMAN.
AH, I'VE MOVED ON FROM "CITIZEN" TO "FINGERMAN." ODD HOW "CITIZEN" HAD MORE WARMTH. WHY AM I HERE? I THOUGHT O'BILEY -- UH, I MEAN **MODOZ** -- DEEMED ME PERSONA NON GRATA.
YOU WERE TOO FIT TO TURN AWAY.
THIS TAKES ALL THE FUN OUT OF NEW CLOTHES.
"FIT?"
FOR **BREEDING**. CHEEKY OR NOT, YOU'RE A HEALTHY **HUMAN** AND WE NEED THOSE. ARE YOU TWO MARRIED?
YEAH, SO?
THEN YOU CAN SKIP THE MASS WEDDING IN THE CHAPELTORIUM AND GET STRAIGHT TO IT.
"**IT?**" AS IN...?
YES, FINGERMAN, AS IN COITUS.

HEY, LOOK: OUR BAGS ARE BY THE BED. THAT'S VALET SERVICE!
THE BED. AN ACTUAL BED.
WHY DOESN'T IT SURPRISE ME THAT THERE'S A BOMB SHELTER UNDER POX NEWS?
WHATEVER, BOB. A BED. A PRISTINE BED.
WANNA MAKE IT LESS SO?
MY THOUGHT EXACTLY.
IN DEFERENCE TO MY WIFE'S MODESTY I WILL FORGO ANY DEPICTION OF OUR CARNALITY. SUFFICE IT TO SAY THAT WE MUSSED THE SHEETS WITH GUSTO.
SEX ON A MATTRESS. SWEET. NOW I WONDER WHAT THE FOOD SITUATION IS. THINK WE CAN EXPLORE AT WILL?
I DUNNO. DEPENDS ON HOW ORWELLIAN THIS PLACE IS. OR OZ-LIKE.
AND I MEAN THE BUTT-RAPIN' HBO VERSION, NOT THE YELLOW BRICK ROAD ONE. BOY, WIZARD OF OZ, ZARDOZ, OZ THE SHOW. WHAT UP WITH THAT?

DID FOX PRODUCE ANY OF THOSE? I WONDER IF THERE'S STILL INTERNET DOWN HERE?
I HOPE NOT. THAT'S THE BEST THING ABOUT THE APOCALYPSE: **NO COMPUTERS**.
UH, THE DOOR IS **LOCKED**.
UH-OH.
GREETINGS FROM *THE GREAT AND POWERFUL MODOZ*. DON'T WORRY, NEWCOMERS, **THIS IS TEMPORARY**. ROVING PRIVILEGES WILL SOON BE GRANTED. IN THE MEANTIME, ***KEEP ACCLIMATIZING***.
TELERANGER
"ACCLIMATIZING?" IS THAT A EUPHEMISM FOR FUCKING? LET'S HOPE THAT MESSAGE WAS PRERECORDED.
YEAH. AND AUTOMATED.
IF NOT, **THEY'RE WATCHING US**. WE'VE PROVIDED OUR HOSTS WITH CLOSED-CIRCUIT **LIVE PORN**.
YUCCH. I DON'T EVEN WANNA **THINK** ABOUT IT.

AFTER ABOUT A WEEK OR TWO -- IT WAS HARD TO TELL CONFINED IN A WINDOWLESS CELL -- WE WERE RELEASED FROM CAPTIVE COPULATION BY ANOTHER DOUGHY WARDER WITH A SKIN CONDITION.
AND HOW ARE WE ENJOYING OUR ACCOM-MODATIONS, FOLKS?
IT'S COMFORTABLE BUT A TAD CLAUSTROPHOBIC. LIKE IF DAYS INN AND A SUPERMAX PRISON HAD A BABY.
THE BABY BUNKER. VERY GOOD.
BON APPETIT, FOLKS.
THANKS.
HOLY MOLY: KARL AND LYSA ARE HERE!
I CAN'T BELIEVE YOU GUYS ARE HERE. THIS IS INCREDIBLE.
NO KIDDING!
WOW. WOW. I WONDER IF ANYONE ELSE WE KNEW BEFORE IS STILL ALIVE.
YEAH, SEEING YOU GUYS IS A HOPEFUL SIGN.
HEY, NO CUTTING!

CUTTING LINE. ≥TSK≤
OH FER CRYIN' OUT LOUD. FINE, GO. BE OUR GUESTS.
AMAZING. EVEN NOW PEOPLE SWEAT THIS STUFF.
SO, YOU GUYS TRAVEL HERE OR WERE YOU OUT OF HOBOKEN ANYWAY?
WE WERE HERE, FOR HOWEVER LONG IT'S BEEN. WE FELL IN WITH SOME NICE MUTANTS, THOUGH.
SAME HERE! AND ZOMBIES!
REANIMATED-AMERICANS, SWEETIE. I MISS ALL THOSE GUYS. I HOPE THEY'RE OKAY.
THIS IS ALL PRETTY WEIRD. I NEVER THOUGHT I'D BE LIVING IN A BUNKER BEING OSTENSIBLY FORCED TO, UM, TRY AND MAKE BABIES.
YEAH. LIKE I NEEDED AN EXCUSE.
BUT DIDN'T YOU HAVE A VAS--
SMAP!
A VAST COLLECTION OF COMICS? WHY YES.

(IX-NAY ON THE ASECTOMY-VAY. **THEY** DON'T NEED TO KNOW THAT.)
OOPS. YEAH, SORRY ABOUT YOUR "COMIC BOOK COLLECTION." JEEZ, THINKING ABOUT THAT, I NEVER MOURNED MY ARMY OF TOY SUPERMANS.
YEAH. CHRIST, MY BOOKS. MY DVDS. MY TOYS. MY ART. ALL GONE.
THE WORLD ENDS, NO TEARS.
BUT THEIR COLLECTIBLES? SUDDENLY THE WATERWORKS.
MEN.
HEY, I MISS MY BOOKS. THE ONLY TWO IN OUR ROOM ARE *THE BIBLE* -- WHICH WE KEEP TRYING TO RID OURSELVES OF AND THEY KEEP BRINGING BACK -- AND A NICHOLAS SPARKS. *YUCCH*.
WHICH ONE?
DOES IT MATTER? WHAT'S REALLY GETTING TO ME ARE THE INDOCTRINATION VIDEOS FEATURING O'BILEY. I MEAN "MODOZ."
I KNOW WHAT YOU MEAN. AND YOU CAN'T MUTE OR ANYTHING.
BOB'S GRINDING HIS TEETH ALL NIGHT. THEY'LL BE DOWN TO NUBS SOON.
IT'S THE MOST MESSED-UP SCENARIO EVER. SEX ALL THE TIME IS GREAT, BUT ENDURING ENDLESS MODOZ VIDEOS? *YEESH.*
UH-OH. SPEAK OF THE DEVIL...

ALL RISE FOR THE GREAT AND OMNISCIENT MODOZ!
GREETINGS, ALL. WELCOME TO THE GRAND DINING HALL OF *THE COUNCIL OF MODOZ*. I'M GLAD YOU'VE ALL HAD A CHANCE TO, *HEH-HEH*, MAKE YOURSELVES *COMFORTABLE* IN PURSUIT OF THE GREATER GOOD.
I SHOULDN'T BE YOUR NATIVE BEARER. THE "**PAPA BEAR**" THING WAS A **JOKE**.
SILENCE, YOU!
ANYWAY, FOLKS, YOU'VE ALL BEEN DOING A **BANG-UP JOB**. SENSORS IN YOUR CHAMBERS INDICATE A HIGH LEVEL OF **PROCREATIVE ACTIVITY**.
OH **GOD**, THEY **HAVE** BEEN **WATCHING** US. I'M GONNA BE **SICK**.

BUT SOME OF YOU ARE TOO MUCH INTO RECREATIVE ACTIVITY.
REMEMBER THE MOTTO FROM COM-VID 32, PULLING OUT: THE TRAITOR'S GAMBIT: "BACKS ARE FOR SCRATCHING, NOT SPLATTERING." UNLESS YOU'RE INTO MISSIONARY, IN WHICH CASE SUBSTITUTE "BELLIES" FOR "BACKS."
(I NEVER THOUGHT A CYBORG RILE O'BILEY WOULD BE LECTURING ME ON THE UNPATRIOTIC NATURE OF MONEY SHOTS.)
IT'S A FALLEN WORLD.
OTHERS OF YOU HAVE DELIBERATELY DECEIVED. MODOZ TRIED TO BE BENEVOLENT, BUT YOU KNOW HOW SOME PEOPLE ARE, FOLKS. SOME FOLKS DON'T SCAN WHEN YOU SCAN 'EM.
(UH-OH.)

BY OTHERS I MEAN YOU, FINGERMAN! NO ROOM FOR PINHEADED PUNKS SHOOTING BLANKS IN THE BABY BUNKER!
DID HE HEAR ME? HE COULDN'T HAVE HEARD ME!
AND TO THINK I WHISPERED IN PIG LATIN FOR NAUGHT.
YOUR FRIEND DIDN'T GIVE ANYTHING AWAY, PINHEAD! I, THE GREAT AND POWERFUL MODOZ, FINALLY DETECTED A TINY BIT OF TITANIUM IN YOUR PERSON!
SO?
OH NUTS.
EXACTLY. THE VASCLIP IN YOUR MAN-SAC. GUARDS, TAKE HIM AWAY!
LET THIS BE A LESSON TO ALL! HA HA HA HA HA!

DON'T MAKE BABIES WITH ANYONE, SWEETIE!
YOU BE STRONG, YOU SURVIVE... YOU STAY ALIVE, NO MATTER WHAT OCCURS!
BOB! NO! BOB!
DID HE JUST QUOTE LAST OF THE MOHICANS?
PEOPLE SAY STRANGE THINGS WHEN THEY'RE STRESSED.
BOB...
DON'T SEPARATE ME FROM MY WIFE, HAZMAT GUY. PLEASE! I THOUGHT WE WERE PALS.
SORRY, CITIZEN, JUST FOLLOWING ORDERS.
YOU'D HAVE MADE A GREAT NAZI.
THAT HURTS, CITIZEN.

AND OUT YOU GO. MEET **MONGO**, YOUR **NEW WIFE!** ROTSA RUCK.
TAKE YOUR CLOTHES OFF.
EVEN WITH THINGS GOING ALL *THUNDER-DOME/DELIVERANCE* ON ME, I VOWED TO GET BACK TO MICHELE, BUTT-CHERRY INTACT, SAVE HER AND EXACT SERIOUS PAYBACK.

WHATTAYA MEAN "TAKE YOUR CLOTHES OFF"? **WHY?**
YOU'RE NOT DRESSED FOR WHAT WE HAVE TO DO.
LATER FOR YOU, CITIZEN-ROMEO.
I **DON'T** LIKE THE LOOKS OF **THAT**. WHAT **IS** THAT **THING**? SOME KIND OF **RAPE-SPEAR?**
LIKE THE PLAYWRIGHT?
HUH?
THE BARD OF AVON?
THAT'S SHAKESPEARE.
ISN'T THAT WHAT YOU SAID?

I SAID RAPE SPEAR.
OH. OOOH. YUCK. NO. NO, IT'S A HOLE DIGGER. FOR PLANTING. YUCK. RAPE SPEAR? THAT'S SICK.
YOU HEARD SHAKESPEARE?
I CAN'T HEAR SO WELL. CAULIFLOWER EARS, DON'TCHA KNOW? I'M CUBBY, BY THE WAY.
CUBBY?
MY GREENISH COMPLEXION AND BUMPY NOGGIN. IT'S A NICKNAME. CUBBY, AS IN BROCCOLI.
THEY SAID YOUR NAME WAS MONGO.
AH, THOSE GUYS ARE JERKS. NOW TAKE YOUR CLOTHES OFF. THOSE DR. DENTON'S WON'T CUT IT OUT HERE.
SO, MAN-RAPE ISN'T ON THE MENU?
DISAPPOINTED? NO, WORSE: PLANTATION WORK. HERE'S YOUR OLD CLOTHING. THEY SAID YOU WANTED THE PANTS.
OMIGOD, THAT DUDE WAS RIGHT! THEY SMELL LIKE 31 FLAVORS OF ASS.
AFTER A DAY IN THE FIELD YOU WON'T SMELL ANYTHING ANY MORE.

TIME TO MEET THE OTHERS. GANG, THIS IS BOB. BOB, THESE ARE--
FUCK ME SIDEWAYS, YOU ARE A **HEINOUS ABOMINATION.** I MEAN, NICE TO MEET YOU.
I **AM** A WAKING NIGHTMARE, AREN'T I? BUT I AM **STRONG.** I COULD BENCH A **SEMI.** WHAT CAN **YOU** DO, **PERSON?**
WOW. NEVER HAS THE WORD "**PERSON**" DRIPPED WITH SO MUCH DISDAIN. UNLESS **I** SAID IT.
HEY, I MEANT NO OFFEN--
YOU AND THAT TOURETTE'S-LIKE FRANKNESS.

BYRON! WOW! YOU'RE HERE!
GOOD TO SEE YOU, TOO, BUDDY. YEAH, THEY ROUNDED UP ALL US MUTIES AND PUT US TO WORK.
WELCOME TO SLAVERY TWO-POINT-OH: NEW, IMPROVED, COLOR-BLIND.
KPOW!
WARNING SHOT EQUALS BACK TO WORK. UGH.
REAP, SOW, REAP, SOW. I HAVE AN MBA FOR CHRIST'S SAKES. THIS SUCKS.
AS THE OTHERS SHOWED ME THE ROPES IN THE FIELDS, MICHELE HAD HER OWN HELL TO DEAL WITH. MAYBE IT'S UNORTHODOX IN A MEMOIR TO SWITCH NARRATORS, BUT TAG TEAM IT SHALL BE AS I LET HER TAKE OVER FOR HER PARTS OF THE STORY.
So, Bob was thrown out and I was freaking out. They didn't tell me what they were going to do. For all I knew Bob had a date with a firing squad. It's not like they hadn't shot people before.
I DOUBT THEY'LL SHOOT BOB. HE'S A HEALTHY SPECIMEN.
HIS MOUTH IS HIS HEALTHIEST ORGAN.
UH, T.M.I., SWEETIE.
NO, NO, NO. NOT LIKE THAT. WELL, ACTUALLY, YEAH LIKE THAT. BUT NO, I MEAN HE RUNS HIS MOUTH AND GETS IN TROUBLE. INSERT FOOT. THAT KIND OF THING.

HE AND KARL SHARE THAT AFFLICTION.
ANYWAY, IT WASN'T HIS **MOUTH** THAT GOT HIM OUSTED. AND IF THERE'S A FIRING SQUAD IN BOB'S FUTURE ***THEY*** WON'T BE SHOOTING BLANKS.
NOW, NOW. YOUR HUSBAND HAS JUST BEEN PUT TO WORK GROWING FOOD FOR US TO EAT.
HE HAD GOTTEN PRETTY GOOD AT PLANTING SEEDS.
DEARIE, IF HE'D BEEN ANY GOOD AT **THAT** HE WOULDN'T BE IN THIS PICKLE.
SPEAKING OF WHICH, WE'LL NEED TO START WORKING ON GETTING YOU IN THE **FAMILY WAY**. I'LL BE LEAVIN' YOU TO YOUR GRIEVIN', BUT SOON, DEARIE. **SOON.**
WAIT A SEC! ***WHAT? BOB'S GONE.*** *WHATTAYA MEAN "****FAMILY WAY****"?*
WELL, WE CAN'T HAVE YOU **BOTH** USELESS TO MODOZ'S REPOPULATION DIRECTIVE.
WE NEED A **BABY** IN YOUR **TUMMY**, LICKETY-SPLIT.
ARE YOU FUCKING KIDDING ME?

I DON'T KID, DEARIE. AND MIND YOUR LANGUAGE. I DON'T BROOK ANY BACKSASS FROM THE FILLIES IN MY STABLE.
NOW GET SOME REST, COLLECT YOURSELF AND WE'LL GET YOU BACK ON TRACK, DEARIE. NIGHTY-NIGHT.
As my pillowy warder waddled off with her warning rattling around in my head, the chorus of one of my favorite Police songs began to leak out of my mouth...
BED'S TOO BIG WITHOUT YOU / THE BED'S TOO BIG WITHOUT YOU / THE BED'S TOO BIG / WITHOUT YOOOU...

MOST. BACK. BREAKING. DAY. EVER.
YOU'LL BE FINE. THE FIRST FEW WERE THE WORST. ACTUALLY, IT'S ALWAYS BAD.
SIGH I MISS MICHELE.
DON'T GET ALL GOOEY LOOKING AT MY DIRTY PILLOWS, DUDE.
I HAVE TO GET BACK TO HER. **HAVE** TO. I CAN'T JUST LEAVE HER IN THERE.
DUDE, **SHE'S** GOT IT **GOOD** IN THERE.
HOW WOULD **YOU** KNOW? **I** WAS IN THERE. SURE, THEY FEED YOU REGULARLY AND YOU GET TO CANOODLE ALL DAY LONG, BUT IT'S, UM...
YEAH, IT SOUNDS HORRIBLE.
A PRISON BY ANY OTHER NAME, YOU DIG? IT'S CALLED "THE **BABY** BUNKER." **THAT'S** WHY THEY PITCHED ME OUT.
IMPOTENT?
HE'S **NOT** IMPOTENT. DON'T YOU REMEMBER ALL THE RUTTING NOISE FROM THEIR HUT?

THAT'S EMBARRASSING. ANYWAY, THEY FOUND OUT I HAD A VASECTOMY BUT MICHELE'S STILL IN THERE AND--
OH JEEZ.
EXACTLY. I HAVE THIS PARADE OF SUITORS BOBBING THROUGH MY HEAD. THIS ENDLESS LINEUP OF WIENERS FULL OF MOTILE SPERM.
HEY, SOME OF US ARE TRYING TO EAT PHALLIC VEGETABLES HERE. YOU MIND?
IN MY HEAD IS THIS PORNOGRAPHIC VERSION OF THE OLD "LET'S ALL GO TO THE LOBBY" ANIMATION...
...ONLY INSTEAD OF POPCORN BOXES AND SODA CUPS IT'S A BUNCH OF VEINY PECKERS.
LET'S GO INTO VAGINA / LET'S GO INTO VAGINA / LET'S GO INTO VAGINA AND GET MICHELE PREG-NANT!
HE'S FLIPPED. MUST BE DELIRIUM FROM HARD LABOR. SAD, REALLY.

THIS IS INSANE. THE WORLD'S COME TO AN END AND IT'S WORSE THAN EVER.
HOW COULD IT BE WORSE THAN EVER WHEN IT'S OVER?
BECAUSE IT'S NOT OVER. HERE WE ARE, MUTATED AND BELEAGUERED AND ENSLAVED.
YEAH.
WE'RE ALL IN THIS TOGETHER.
PICTURE YOUR SWEETHEART BEING SERVICED BY A BUNCH OF STRANGE PENISES AND GET BACK TO ME ON THE SHARED EXPERIENCE ANGLE, OKAY?
EW. I DON'T WANT TO THINK ABOUT HER AND ANY PENISES.
ME NEITHER.
OKAY, CAN THE BALLOON JUICE, FOLKS. TIME TO HIT THE BUNKHOUSE FOR SOME ZEES.

UH, DOESN'T BUNKHOUSE INDICATE THERE WILL BE BUNKS? AND A HOUSE?
WHAT'D YOU EXPECT, THE RITZ-CARLTON? IF YOU'D KEPT YOUR 'NADS UN-MONKEYED WITH YOU'D STILL BE IN THE BUNKER WITH YOUR MISSUS.
THAT'S COLD.
AND TO THINK I USED TO LIKE YOU.
I'VE NEVER MET YOU BEFORE.
AH, YOU GUYS ALL LOOK ALIKE TO ME.
HOW VERY UN-P.C. OF YOU. YOU LIBERALS REALLY ARE THE PARTY OF HATE.
ONLY BUNK IN THIS BUNKHOUSE IS THIS BUNKHOUSE IS THE BUNK.
SIGH HOW DO THESE GUYS EVEN KNOW I'M A LIBERAL?
THESE GUYS HAVE GOT DOSSIERS ON ALL OF US.
THEN HOW COME THEY EVEN LET ME IN THERE?

MAYBE TO SCREW WITH YOU. GET YOU THINKING YOU'VE GOT THE LIFE OF RILEY -- OR O'BILEY -- THEN TAKE IT ALL AWAY. ALL YOU HAD LEFT WAS MICHELE AND NOW YOU DON'T EVEN HAVE THAT.
SHE'S ALL I EVER WANTED, ANYWAY.
GET SOME SLEEP, BOBBY. GET SOME SLEEP.
After a sleepless night -- and I never have trouble falling asleep, but circumstances being what they were I tossed and turned and stared at the ceiling -- I was escorted by two of the bunker lackeys to the drabbest battleship gray office ever.
AS YOU'RE ON HIATUS FROM THE PRIME DIRECTIVE, NAMELY MAKING BABIES, WE'VE GOT TO KEEP YOU BUSY.
IT SAYS HERE THAT YOU WERE IN PERSONNEL.
HUMAN RESOURCES.
YES, WELL. TO-MATO, TO-MAHTO. WE NEED YOU TO ADMINISTER THE POPULATION OF THE BUNKER.

YOU'VE GOT TO BE KIDDING. I WAS FINALLY FREE, HAPPY AS A PIG IN SHIT DOING GARDENING, AND NOW *THIS?*
YOU NEED TO BE **PRO**DUCTIVE UNTIL YOU GET **REPRO**DUCTIVE. THEN YOU'LL BE EARNING YOUR KEEP.
SO IT'S WORK IN HERE OR LET YOU KNOCK ME UP WITH SOME STRANGER'S JIZZ?
YOU HAVE QUITE THE MOUTH ON YOU. BUT YES, WORK HERE OR MAKE BABIES.
BOB AND I PURPOSEFULLY **DIDN'T** WANT KIDS. CAN'T YOU **RESPECT** THAT?
NO. IF *YOU'RE* MARRIED AND **DON'T** WANT CHILDREN YOU'RE SUPERFICIAL, SHALLOW, HORRIBLE PEOPLE.
DIDN'T JUDGMENTAL POPULAR ENTERTAINMENT TEACH *YOU ANYTHING?*
AND THERE THEY GO, TWEEDLEDUM AND TWEEDLEDEE. GAH-DAMN EUNUCHS. I'M MILLIE.

MICHELE. AND WHY ARE **YOU** HERE? WHAT'S **YOUR** CRIME?
I'M FIFTY-SIX AND DIDN'T HAVE THE DECENCY TO DROP DEAD IN THE FALLOUT. MY WOMB'S A ROCK, HONEY.
OH. WHAT'S THE DEAL WITH **THOSE** GUYS, ANYWAY? THEY ALL--
LOOK LIKE **KARL ROVE?** WHEN THAT LITTLE FAGGOT WAS ATTENDING THE UNIVERSITY OF UTAH, TO GET OUT OF SERVING IN 'NAM HE VOLUNTEERED FOR A HUSH-HUSH CLONING EXPERIMENT.
THE PRIGGISH LITTLE CREEPS AIN'T EXACT COPIES, BUT NEAR ENOUGH.
SERIOUSLY?
SERIOUS AS THE HEART ATTACK I KEEP HOPING FOR. ANYWAY, THE CLONES ARE ALL **NEUTER**. BUT WHAT'S THE DIFF? THERE'S **DOZENS** OF THEM.
HOW DO YOU KNOW ALL THIS?
YOU POKE AROUND YOU CAN FIND THINGS OUT. THESE COMPUTERS, CRUMMY AS THEY ARE, HOLD A WEALTH OF DIRT.
ANY CLUE AS TO WHAT CAUSED ALL THIS?
THE MOST POPULAR THEORY IS BUSH COULDN'T BEAR THE IDEA OF NOT BEING PRESIDENT SO HE AND CHENEY LOOSED THE NUKES FROM THEIR LUXURY SHELTER.
I COULD SEE THAT.
IT'S **JUST** A **THEORY**, KID. WE'LL PROBABLY **NEVER** KNOW.

AREN'T THESE POLES A LITTLE HEAVY-DUTY FOR CROPS?
MUTANT CROPS.
I S'POSE. SHOULDN'T IT BE COLD WEATHER BY NOW? I'M BAKING.
MAYBE ALL THOSE A-BOMBS TIPPED THE PLANET'S AXIS A FRACTION. OR THE OZONE BAKED OFF. WHO KNOWS?
DUDE, I'M SWEATIN' MY TITS OFF.

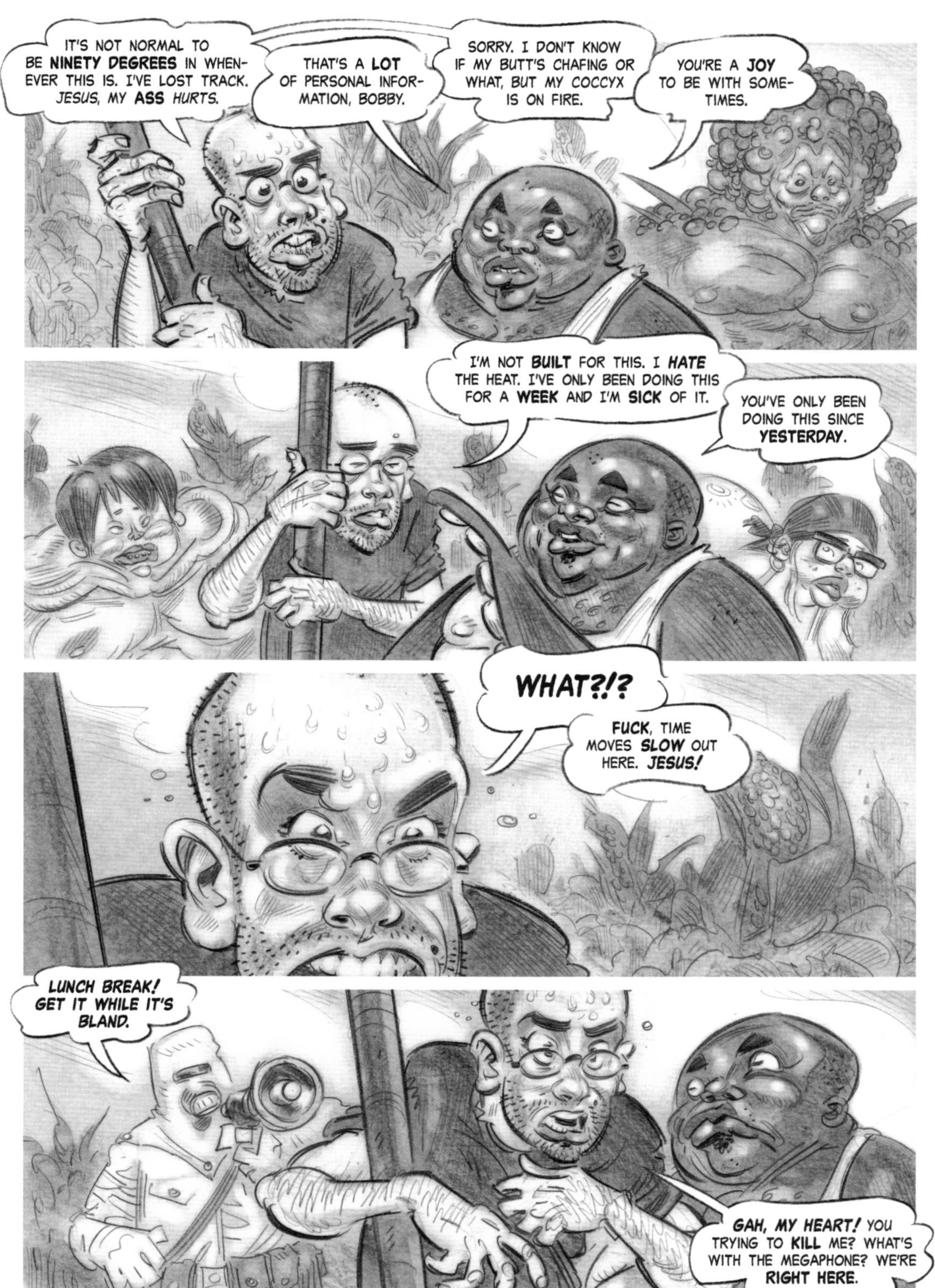
IT'S NOT NORMAL TO BE NINETY DEGREES IN WHENEVER THIS IS. I'VE LOST TRACK. JESUS, MY ASS HURTS.
THAT'S A LOT OF PERSONAL INFORMATION, BOBBY.
SORRY. I DON'T KNOW IF MY BUTT'S CHAFING OR WHAT, BUT MY COCCYX IS ON FIRE.
YOU'RE A JOY TO BE WITH SOMETIMES.
I'M NOT BUILT FOR THIS. I HATE THE HEAT. I'VE ONLY BEEN DOING THIS FOR A WEEK AND I'M SICK OF IT.
YOU'VE ONLY BEEN DOING THIS SINCE YESTERDAY.
WHAT?!?
FUCK, TIME MOVES SLOW OUT HERE. JESUS!
LUNCH BREAK! GET IT WHILE IT'S BLAND.
GAH, MY HEART! YOU TRYING TO KILL ME? WHAT'S WITH THE MEGAPHONE? WE'RE RIGHT HERE.

ARE YOU WEARING A HAIR NET?
IT'S WHIMSICAL. SO, YOU WANT YOUR FOOD OR NOT?
WE GROW FRESH VEGETABLES AND GET THIS TO EAT?
AND IF THEY CATCH US EATING WHAT WE PICK WE GET A BEATING.
IT'S SURE NOT THE SAME AS FRESH.
YOU GUYS: THE FOODIES. S'MATTER, YOU RUN OUT OF TV CHEFS TO NOSH ON?
UGH: THE ENTENMANN'S FAN. CUTE. I THINK WE'VE HAD IT. AWFUL "FOOD." GRUELING LABOR. THE HEAT. IT'S TOO MUCH.
PLUS, I THINK WE'RE RIDDLED WITH CANCERS. THE APOCALYPSE IS CATCHING UP WITH US.
THEY SAY WE'RE NOT FIT TO BREED SO THEY WORK US TO DEATH IN THE FIELDS, BUT LOOK AT YOU: THE PICTURE OF HEALTH. YOU AND YOUR ≥AHEM≤ MUTANT CONFRERES.
YEAH, WELL, GOOD LUCK WITH YOUR DYING AND ALL.

OUCH. WOW, MY BUTT'S TENDER.
I WOULDN'T SAY THAT SO LOUD NEAR THOSE RACIST CANNIBALS.
CHOKING DOWN BRITTLE CRACKERS IN THE PRESENCE OF BRITTLE CRACKERS. THAT'S SYMMETRICAL, I SUPPOSE. I MEAN, EATING PEOPLE IS ONE THING, BUT BIGOTRY? THAT'S SO FIVE MINUTES BEFORE THE APOCALYPSE.
LOOK AT YOU, WITH YOUR BLACK FRIENDS AND YOUR ASIAN FRIENDS AND YOUR LESBIAN FRIENDS.
I DON'T THINK OF YOU GUYS THAT WAY. I JUST THINK OF YOU AS MY HIDEOUSLY DEFORMED MUTANT FRIENDS.
YOU ARE ONE ADORABLE MOTHERFUCKER, YOU KNOW THAT?
YEAH, I KNOW.
Weeks passed in the office. Hours heaped on hours of unrelieved tedium. Even food offered no comfort.
YOU GONNA EAT THAT, HON?
≶SIGH≶ THIS REMINDS ME OF BOB.
LOOK, HON, I LIKE YOU, BUT I DON'T NEED TO KNOW THAT.
WHAT? OH, NO. HA HA. BOB AND I GREW A RUDE CARROT. WE TAUNTED CRAZY CHRISTIANS WITH IT. I WASN'T BEING LEWD.

ON THE OTHER HAND...
RIGHT, HON, BACK TO WORK.
THIS IS SO DEMEANING. I WAS A MANAGING DIRECTOR AT GELDBILDETGELDBANK.
WORK IS WORK, KID. NEVER HAD A CAREER, I JUST HAD JOBS.
THE ONE THING THE APOCALYPSE GAVE ME WAS RELIEF FROM ANY OF THIS. I'M NOT DOING THIS ANYMORE. LET 'EM KEEP THEIR OWN RECORDS STRAIGHT.
I WOULDN'T SAY THAT SO LOUD.
WHY NOT?
FRICK AND FRACK HAVE GREAT EARS.
WE'RE DELIGHTED YOU'VE DECIDED TO GO WITH THE BREEDING INSTEAD.
LEAVE THE FILING TO--
THE OLD BROAD WITH THE WOMB LIKE A TOMB.
NOT HOW I'D HAVE PHRASED IT, BUT YES.
NO, WAIT. I LOVE FILING. THESE COMMODORE 64s OR WHAT-EVER THEY ARE ARE GREAT.

NICE TRY, BUT IT'S BACK TO YOUR CHAMBER TO GET READY FOR BABY-MAKING.
HOORAY.
TOLD YA NOT TO TALK SO LOUD.
WAIT! DON'T DO THIS! I DON'T WANT BABIES! I HAVE NO MATERNAL INSTINCT!
THIS IS BULLSHIT! YOU HEAR ME? THIS IS U.S. GRADE "A" BULLSHIT!
WHO SAYS YOU'D BE RAISING THE CHILD? WE JUST NEED YOU TO HAVE IT. AND THEN ANOTHER AND ANOTHER--
THAT LANGUAGE. SO UNLADYLIKE.
EAT A BOWL OF FUCK, YOU FLACCID CLONES OF A TURD BLOSSOM.
DEFINITELY NOT RAISING THE CHILD.
HOME AGAIN, HOME AGAIN.
SUCK A BAG OF DICKS, YOU BALD-HEADED BLOBS.
LET'S HOPE HER UTERUS HAS BETTER MANNERS THAN SHE DOES.

I AM **SO** FUCKED.
BUT NOT **LITERALLY**, I HOPE.
CLANG!
SO, YOU'VE DECIDED TO MAKE A BABY. CONGRATULATIONS. WELCOME TO COM-VID 12, ***CONCEIVING: THE PATRIOT'S CHOICE***.
NOW, TO GET YOU LADIES IN AN EXTRA FERTILE STATE I'LL READ EROTIC PASSAGES FROM MY NOVEL ***THEY WHO TRANSGRESS***. ⋛AHEM⋚
OH GOD, WHAT THE HELL AM I GOING TO DO?
TELERANGER
"ANDREA JOHNSON REMOVED HER POWDER-BLUE SATIN BLOUSE AND UNHITCHED HER **BRA**. HER UNRESTRAINED **BOSOMS** WERE **BUXOM** AND **SOLID**. SHE SLIPPED A **TEDDY** ON, THE KIND SLENDER MODELS WORE IN THE *FREDERICK'S OF HOLLYWOOD* CATALOG. ANDREA'S **BREASTS** FILLED THE FABRIC, AND HER **NIPPLES**...
⋛SIGH⋚
TELERANGER
With MODOZ's droning purple prose in the background, the prospect of fending off spermy suitors filled me with dread, and dread was about all I'd allow myself to be filled with. I needed Bob. Why couldn't they just evict me, too? I realized that, hardships and all, we'd been happy in the wasteland. I missed our mutant and re-animated buddies, even Caesar. I had to get out of the Baby Bunker.

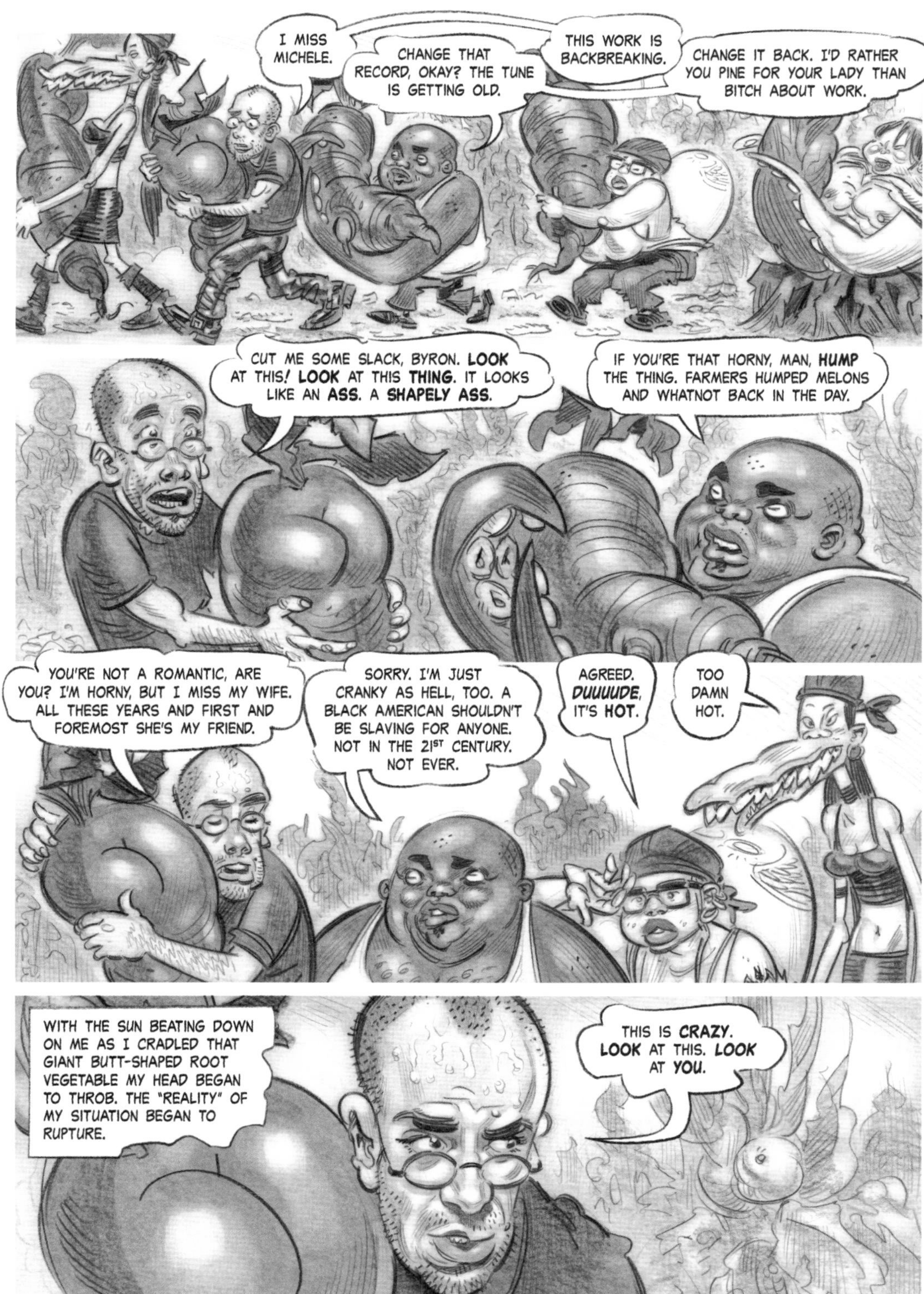
I MISS MICHELE.
CHANGE THAT RECORD, OKAY? THE TUNE IS GETTING OLD.
THIS WORK IS BACKBREAKING.
CHANGE IT BACK. I'D RATHER YOU PINE FOR YOUR LADY THAN BITCH ABOUT WORK.
CUT ME SOME SLACK, BYRON. **LOOK** AT THIS! **LOOK** AT THIS **THING**. IT LOOKS LIKE AN **ASS**. A **SHAPELY ASS**.
IF YOU'RE THAT HORNY, MAN, **HUMP** THE THING. FARMERS HUMPED MELONS AND WHATNOT BACK IN THE DAY.
YOU'RE NOT A ROMANTIC, ARE YOU? I'M HORNY, BUT I MISS MY WIFE. ALL THESE YEARS AND FIRST AND FOREMOST SHE'S MY FRIEND.
SORRY. I'M JUST CRANKY AS HELL, TOO. A BLACK AMERICAN SHOULDN'T BE SLAVING FOR ANYONE. NOT IN THE 21ST CENTURY. NOT EVER.
AGREED. **DUUUUDE**, IT'S **HOT**.
TOO DAMN HOT.
WITH THE SUN BEATING DOWN ON ME AS I CRADLED THAT GIANT BUTT-SHAPED ROOT VEGETABLE MY HEAD BEGAN TO THROB. THE "REALITY" OF MY SITUATION BEGAN TO RUPTURE.
THIS IS **CRAZY**. **LOOK** AT THIS. **LOOK** AT **YOU**.

I MEAN REALLY. TENTACLES FOR ARMS. GOAT'S EYES.
A PERFECT EGG-SHAPED HUMP. AND YOU, WITH THE DISTENDED MAW LIKE AN ALLIGATOR.
AND YOU...
FOR FUCK'S SAKES, LOOK AT YOU. WHAT IS THAT? LITTLE BOY'S HEAD QUEEFED UP ON AN OPEN LABIAL PLATTER OF I DON'T EVEN KNOW WHAT! BRAMBLE LEGS? IT MAKES NO SENSE.

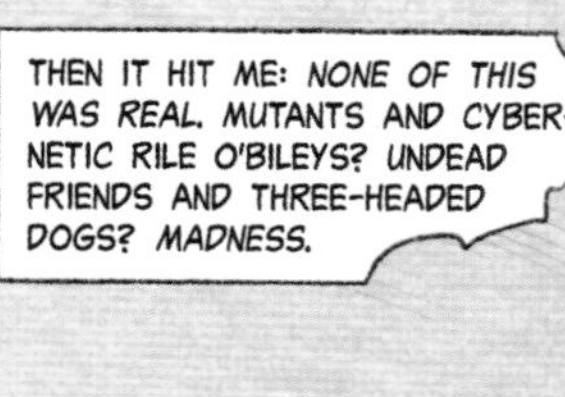
THEN IT HIT ME: *NONE OF THIS WAS REAL*. MUTANTS AND CYBERNETIC RILE O'BILEYS? UNDEAD FRIENDS AND THREE-HEADED DOGS? *MADNESS*.

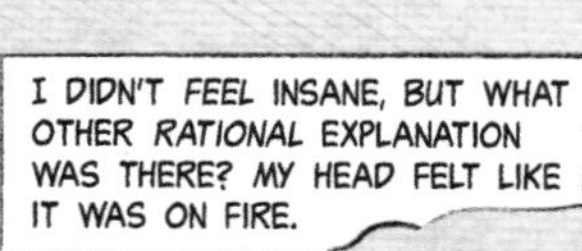
I DIDN'T *FEEL* INSANE, BUT WHAT OTHER *RATIONAL* EXPLANATION WAS THERE? MY HEAD FELT LIKE IT WAS ON FIRE.

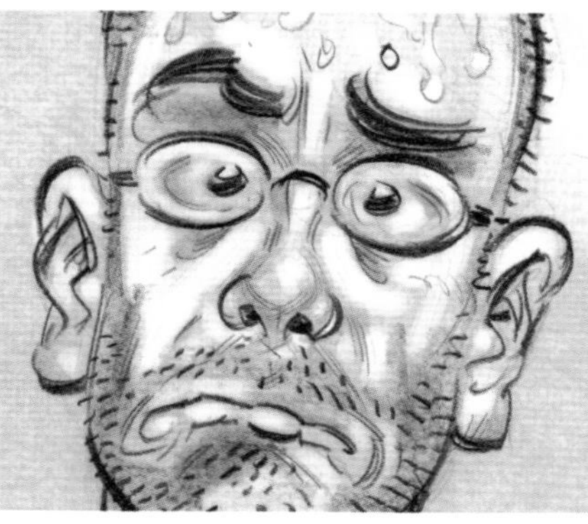
AND THEN IT BEGAN TO MAKE SENSE. IT WAS A REVERIE. THE APOCALYPTIC THEME.
THE INTRODUCTION OF THE SENSE OF LOSS AND SEPARATION.

THERE **HAD** BEEN A NUCLEAR ATTACK, BUT NOT GLOBAL. NOT EPIC. JUST BIG ENOUGH. MAYBE A ***DIRTY BOMB***. THE HEAT I FELT. IT MADE SENSE.
I HAVE A PRETTY VIVID IMAGINATION. THOUGH IT HAD BEEN NEARLY A DECADE SINCE **9/11**, THE CONSTANT DRUMBEAT OF THE SO-CALLED "***WAR ON TERROR***" WAS ALWAYS IN THE BACKGROUND.
THEY'D DONE IT *AGAIN*. NEW YORK IS AND EVER WILL BE TOP OF THE LIST OF TARGETS FOR **TERRORISM**. IT'S ***THE*** HEART OF FINANCE. WASHINGTON HAS THE *POLITICS* BUT **WE** HAVE THE ***MONEY***.

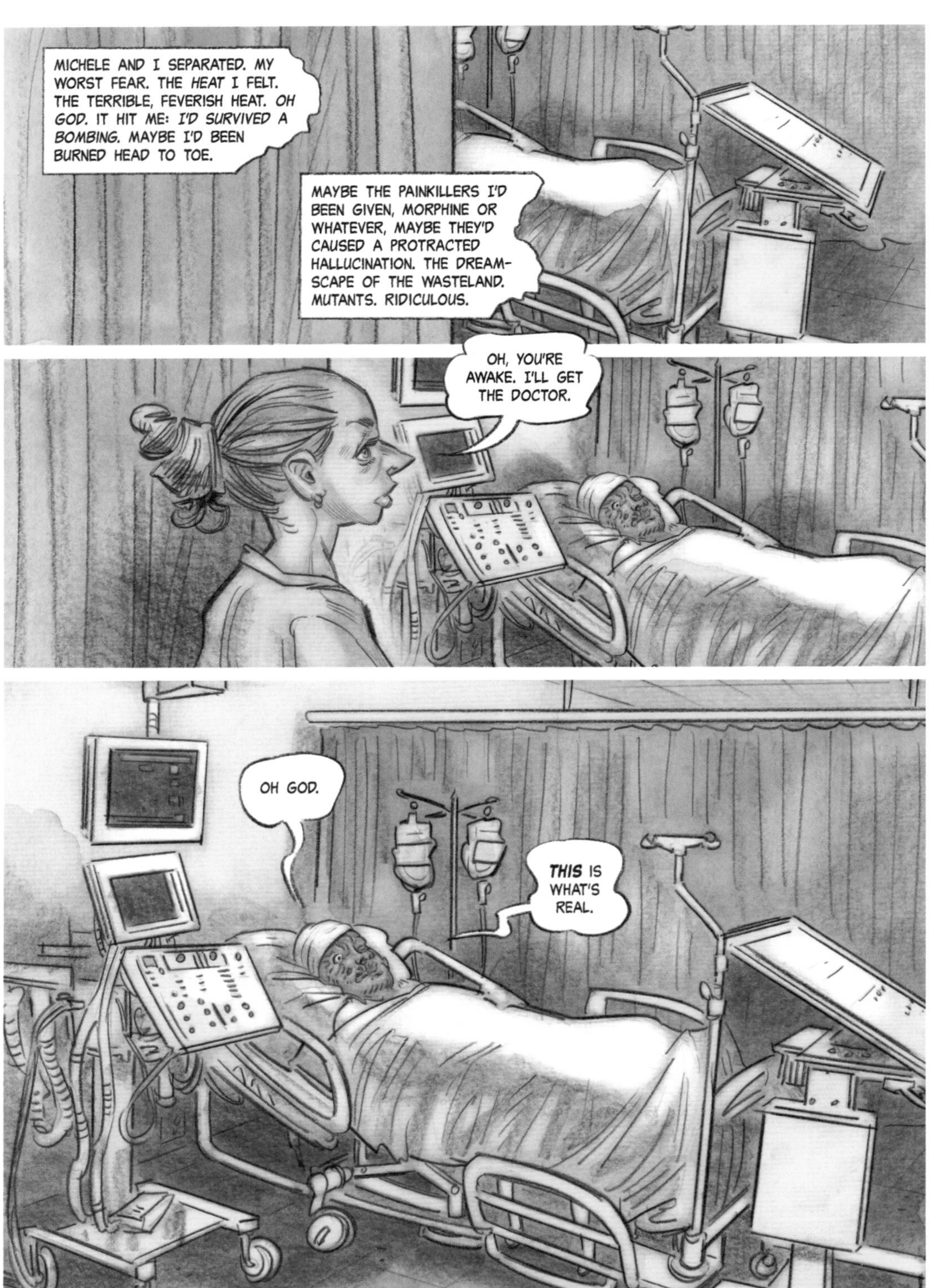
MICHELE AND I SEPARATED. MY WORST FEAR. THE *HEAT* I FELT. THE TERRIBLE, FEVERISH HEAT. *OH GOD.* IT HIT ME: *I'D SURVIVED A BOMBING.* MAYBE I'D BEEN BURNED HEAD TO TOE.
MAYBE THE PAINKILLERS I'D BEEN GIVEN, MORPHINE OR WHATEVER, MAYBE THEY'D CAUSED A PROTRACTED HALLUCINATION. THE DREAM-SCAPE OF THE WASTELAND. MUTANTS. RIDICULOUS.
OH, YOU'RE AWAKE. I'LL GET THE DOCTOR.
OH GOD.
THIS IS WHAT'S REAL.

NEXT THING I KNEW I WAS LYING ON MY BACK, A HAZMAT GUY PULLING A HYPO OUT OF MY CHEST AND BYRON GLARING AT ME. **HEATSTROKE.** I'D ONLY HAD IT ONCE BEFORE, WHEN I WAS A KID IN DISNEY WORLD. LEAVE IT TO ME TO HAVE A DELIRIUM DARKER THAN THE APOCALYPSE.
THIS STIM-SHOT AND AN ICE PACK SHOULD DO THE TRICK.
I WANNA HIT HIM AGAIN. JUST ONE MORE TIME. "TENTACLE ARMS AND GOAT EYES," HE SAYS.
YOU **DO** HAVE **TENTACLE ARMS** AND **GOAT EYES.** AND **I** HAVE A **BIG-ASS HUMP.**
I HATE TO ADMIT IT, BUT I DO LOOK LIKE **WALLY GATOR**, ONLY NOT AS CUTE.
YOU'LL ALWAYS LOOK CUTE TO ME, BABY.

AND THEN THE FEVER BROKE AND I REALIZED THIS WAS REAL. CRAZY AS IT ALL SEEMED MY VISION OF ME IN THE HOSPITAL -- ALONE, AFRAID AND FRICASSEED -- WAS JUST A NIGHTMARISH FANTASY BROUGHT ON BY SUNSTROKE.
WHAT A RELIEF! I'M SO GLAD TO SEE YOU GUYS.
WHO, US? THE FREAKS? YOU REALLY HURT LARRY'S FEELINGS.
WHO'S LARRY?
WHO'S LA--? WOW, THAT'S COLD.
LARRY'S THE MUSCLE-BOUND KID WITH THE BRIAR PATCH LEGS.
I'LL APOLOGIZE LATER. JEEZ, I REALLY HAD MY P.K.D. MOMENT.
P.K.D.?
PHILIP K. DICK. I'D SAY, "GOOGLE IT," BUT NEVER MIND. ANYWAY, IT'S GOOD TO BE BACK, SORT OF.
THIS HARD LABOR'S GONNA KILL ME. LITERALLY. THIS CAN'T GO ON. WE NEED TO TALK.
ARE YOU BREAKING UP WITH US?
IT'S NOT ONE OF THOSE "WE NEED TO TALK" TALKS. OH, RIGHT: SARCASM. I'M A BIT WOOZY.
NOT NOW, BUT LATER, AT THE COUGH "BUNK-HOUSE."
BECAUSE THAT'S SO PRIVATE.
WHATEVER. I'LL WHISPER.

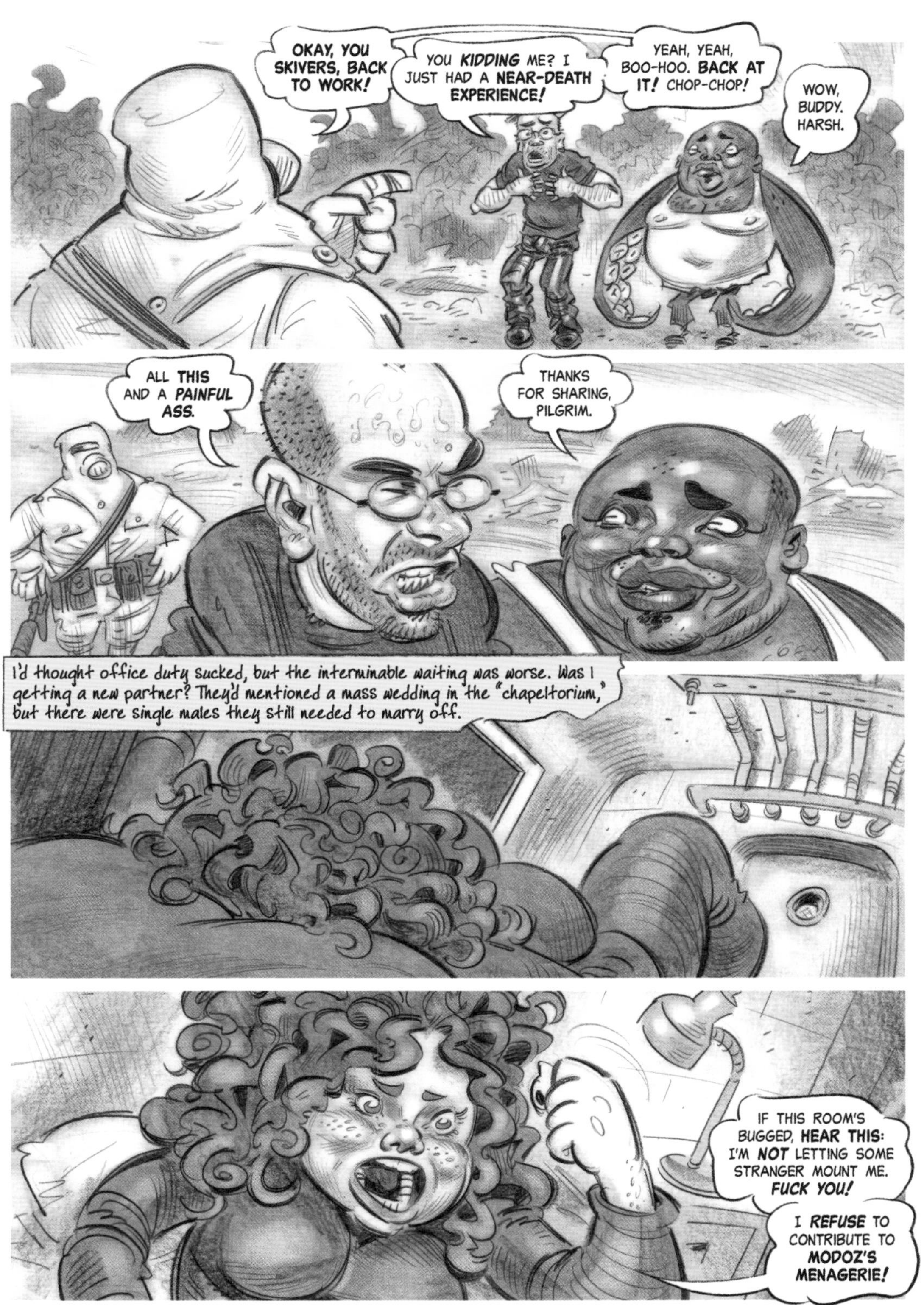
OKAY, YOU SKIVERS, BACK TO WORK!
YOU KIDDING ME? I JUST HAD A NEAR-DEATH EXPERIENCE!
YEAH, YEAH, BOO-HOO. BACK AT IT! CHOP-CHOP!
WOW, BUDDY. HARSH.
ALL THIS AND A PAINFUL ASS.
THANKS FOR SHARING, PILGRIM.
I'd thought office duty sucked, but the interminable waiting was worse. Was I getting a new partner? They'd mentioned a mass wedding in the "chapeltorium," but there were single males they still needed to marry off.
IF THIS ROOM'S BUGGED, HEAR THIS: I'M NOT LETTING SOME STRANGER MOUNT ME. FUCK YOU!
I REFUSE TO CONTRIBUTE TO MODOZ'S MENAGERIE!

CAN'T EVEN FORCE A CONFRONTATION. I NEVER KNEW I COULD BE SIMULTANEOUSLY ANXIOUS AND BORED.
I felt like one of those pandas they used to try to breed in captivity. Soon the impregnation squad would arrive.
I NEED A DETERRENT.
THERE'S GOTTA BE SOMETHING USEFUL IN HERE.
HMMM. I DUNNO...

I'M JUST GLAD YOU'RE NOT MAD, LARRY.
IT'S OKAY, PERSON. YOU HAD A MELT-DOWN.
TRUE. YOU KEEP CALLING ME "PERSON." AREN'T **YOU** A PERSON, TOO?
OUR WARDERS DON'T SEEM TO THINK SO. I THINK MUTANTS ARE MORE THAN THAT NOW.
MAYBE SO.
DEFINITELY SO. **LOOK** AT THEM. THEY WEAR PROTECTIVE GEAR 'CAUSE THEY HAVEN'T ADAPTED.
BEFORE THE FIREWORKS I WAS A SCRAWNY LITTLE BOY. NOW I AM A MIGHTY NEW LIFE FORM.
THE FINE YOUNG CANNIBALS AREN'T LOOKING TOO FINE, EITHER.
IT'S PURE DARWINISM. THEY ARE **NOT** FIT FOR THIS ALTERED WORLD.

FUCK. I CAN'T TAKE THIS ANY MORE. MY ASS IS KILLING ME!
KINDA LOOKS LIKE YOU TOOK THE WORLD'S BIGGEST DUMP IN YOUR DRAWERS, SON.
THAT'S IT! I NEED RELIEF!
LOOKS LIKE YOU ALREADY GOT SOME.
OH, THAT'S BETTER.
I TAKE IT BACK: YOU'RE NOT A PERSON.
WHAT? I CAN'T SEE DICK.
ACTUALLY, THAT'S ALL WE SEE.
WELL, I'LL BE A MONKEY'S UNCLE.
YOU GOT THE TAIL FOR IT, HOSS.
HE'S ONE OF US.
IF ANY OF YOU START CHANTING "GOOBLE-GOBBLE" I'LL FUCKING BRAIN YOU.

HOW ARE YOU HOLDING UP?
LOUSY. I THOUGHT I WAS CONFINED TO QUARTERS, BUT I GUESS THEY'LL LET ME OUT FOR MEALS. I DUNNO.
IT'S VERY BIG OF YOU ASSHOLES TO LET ME OUT TO EAT!
UH, MAYBE YOU SHOULD SIT DOWN AND EAT.
MEH. FOOD'S PROBABLY LACED WITH FERTILITY DRUGS. THEY'RE TRYING TO TURN US INTO BROOD SOWS.
YOU THINK?
EXCUSE ME, MISS, BUT IS THIS SEAT FREE?
NO IT ISN'T. SCREW OFF. YOU'RE NOT GETTIN' IN MY JAMMIES, JERKWAD.
I WASN'T--
YEAH, YEAH. TALK TO THE HAND, RAPEY THE CLOWN. THE HAND AT THE OTHER END OF THE HALL.

IF YOU'RE TRYING THE INSANITY PLOY TO AVOID COPULATION, GOOD JOB.
WE'LL SEE. AS LONG AS MY OVARIES AREN'T NUTS THEY'LL BE WANTING TO DOUSE MY EGGS WITH BABY SAUCE.

CHOOARRRK!
HUUAUUCHHH!
THAT'S APPETIZING.
JESUS CHRIST!
SIGH THEY'RE PROBABLY MY FUTURE "MYSTERY DATES."
OKAY, FOLKS, COMMUNAL DINING IS CANCELED FOR THE EVENING. NOTHING TO SEE HERE.
PLEASE TAKE YOUR MEALS AND RETURN TO YOUR QUARTERS.

YOU NOTICE HOW UNWELL SOME OF THE FOLKS IN HERE LOOK? I'D SAY A GOOD FIFTH OF THE PEOPLE IN HERE LOOK PRETTY IFFY.
MAYBE IT'S MORNING SICK-NESS.
BUT THOSE WERE MEN WHO BARFED.
THAT NIGHT, IN HUSHED VOICES, WE BEGAN TO HATCH A PLAN.
THANKS FOR ALTERING MY PANTS, CINDY. MUCH COMFIER NOW WITH A TAIL HOLE.
NO PROB', DUDE. S'FUNNY YOU'RE A MUTANT, BARELY. I'D SWAP A TAIL FOR THIS BALLOON ON MY BACK.
BALLOON. INTERESTING. YOU MIND?
MIND WHAT?
I'VE NEVER TOUCHED YOUR BACK.
KNOCK YOURSELF OUT, DUDE.
IT'S SOFT AND FEELS... HOLLOW. DO YOU THINK IT COULD BE DEFLATED? OR, UM, INFLATED?
DUNNO. I'M KIND OF AFRAID TO TRY.
WHAT'RE YOU THINKING, BOBBY?

WAY I SEE IT, WE HAVE TWO CHOICES: *CONQUEST OF THE PLANET OF THE APES* OR *THE GREAT ESCAPE.* I'M NOT MUCH FOR FIGHTING.
YEAH, YOU DON'T STRIKE ME AS THE **NAT TURNER** TYPE, THOUGH A **SLAVE REVOLT** APPEALS.
WE **DO** HAVE THE **BRAWN** ADVANTAGE.
FELLAS, I'M A **PACIFIST**. I WAS WORKING ON MY MASTERS IN **LIBRARY SCIENCE**.
HOW DID I NOT NOTICE HOW **SQUISHY** YOUR HUMP WAS?
'CAUSE OF MY LADY LUMPS. ANYWAY, **THEY'VE** GOT THE **GUN** ADVANTAGE.
IF ONLY VIC WAS HERE.
HELIUM VIC?
THEY ROUNDED HIM AND FLOPPY ALAN UP A WHILE BACK. THEY'RE ON **K.P. DUTY**.
K.P.? INSIDE THE BUNKER?
NO MUTIES ALLOWED. RIGHT OUT-SIDE IT. WHY?

After more puking incidents in the mess hall we were finally confined to quarters. To pass time I read the icky prose of Nickle-ass Sparks, fretted about being forcibly impregnated and listened to MODOZ's puerile "erotica." But even that stopped, replaced by matronly hectoring from Ma Rove.
GREETINGS, MODOZTHLICS. THE GREAT MODOZ IS GRAVELY DISAPPOINTED. SINCE THE INCEPTION OF THE CONCEPTION INITIATIVE THERE HAVE BEEN ZERO PREGNANCIES.
GREAT. THIS.
TELERANGER
WE KNOW YOU RANDY BUGGERS ARE COPULATING, BUT TRY HARDER! HAVE YOU SEEN ANY CHILDREN IN THE BUNKER? NO. BECAUSE THERE ARE NONE. NOR THE ELDERLY. BOTH EXTREMES OF THE SPECTRUM WERE ELIMINATED IN THE KERFUFFLE.
WE NEED NEW LIFE. EXTREME TIMES, PEOPLE, EXTREME MEASURES. GOOD NIGHT.
TELERANGER
EXTREME MEASURES? I DO NOT LIKE THE SOUND OF THAT.
I'd noticed the zero tolerance policy re mutants in the bunker. They were deemed useful in growing our food, but they were not welcome.

Extreme measures. "Vagina dentata." That would be pretty mutanty. But the thought of trying to wedge those choppers into my hooha?

I clenched my teeth, girded my loins, swallowed my pride and unzipped my onesie, but...
ZZZZZZZZZIIIIIIIIIIIIIIIIIIIIP...

Nope. I just couldn't do it. It was too fucking gross.
≷SIGH≶ I'LL JUST HAVE TO DISSUADE ANY SPERMY SWAINS ANOTHER WAY.

OH SHIT. SPEAK OF THE DEVIL!
HI, I'M HERE TO--

OH, NO YOU'RE NOT!
UFF!
THWUD!
YOU'RE NOT STICKING YOUR DICK IN ME, CASANOVA.
≷UGH≶ WE'RE NOT... ANIMALS. EVER HEAR OF... ≷UNGH≶... ARTIFICIAL INSEMINATION? ANYWAY, ≷URGH≶ I WAS JUST HERE TO COLLECT YOUR DIRTY DISHES. ≷GROAN≶
OH WELL, FUCK IT.
LATER, SKATER!

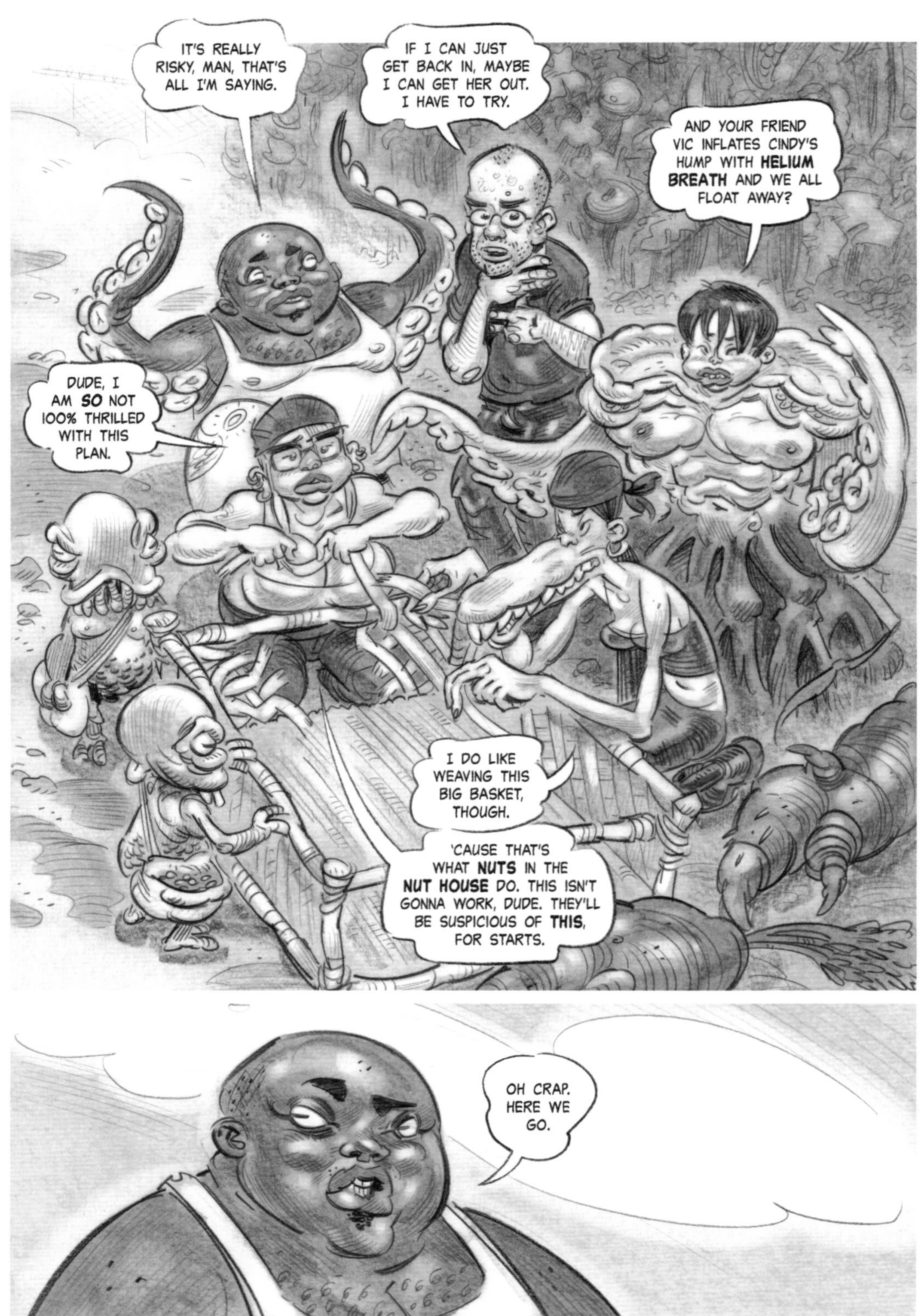
IT'S REALLY RISKY, MAN, THAT'S ALL I'M SAYING.
IF I CAN JUST GET BACK IN, MAYBE I CAN GET HER OUT. I HAVE TO TRY.
AND YOUR FRIEND VIC INFLATES CINDY'S HUMP WITH **HELIUM BREATH** AND WE ALL FLOAT AWAY?
DUDE, I AM **SO** NOT 100% THRILLED WITH THIS PLAN.
I DO LIKE WEAVING THIS BIG BASKET, THOUGH.
'CAUSE THAT'S WHAT **NUTS** IN THE **NUT HOUSE** DO. THIS ISN'T GONNA WORK, DUDE. THEY'LL BE SUSPICIOUS OF **THIS**, FOR STARTS.
OH CRAP. HERE WE GO.

OI, WHAT'S ALL THIS THEN?
IT'S A HAMPER FOR CONVEYING CROPS MORE EFFICIENTLY.
AH. VERY ENTERPRISING. I LIKE YOUR CAN-DO SPIRIT. CARRY ON.
LIKE THE PLAN A LITTLE BETTER?
EXCEPT FOR THE BIT ABOUT BEING INFLATED LIKE A HELIUM BALLOON AND THE LIKELI-HOOD OF THEM SHOOTING US DOWN, YES.
THERE IS THAT POSSIBILITY. MAYBE WE COULD MAKE SOME BOMBS OR SOMETHING.
UH-OH. SOMEONE IS GETTING HIS NAT TURNER ON.
I WAS STUDYING CHEMICAL ENGINEERING BEFORE ALL THIS.
THANK YOU, MR. NON SEQUITUR. ANYWAY, YOU'RE LIKE TEN, KID.
ELEVEN. BUT SMART. HOME SCHOOLED. I HAD BIG DREAMS FOR A CAREER IN ARTIFICIAL FOOD FLAVORING.
KID WAS A FREAK BEFORE ALL THIS WENT DOWN.

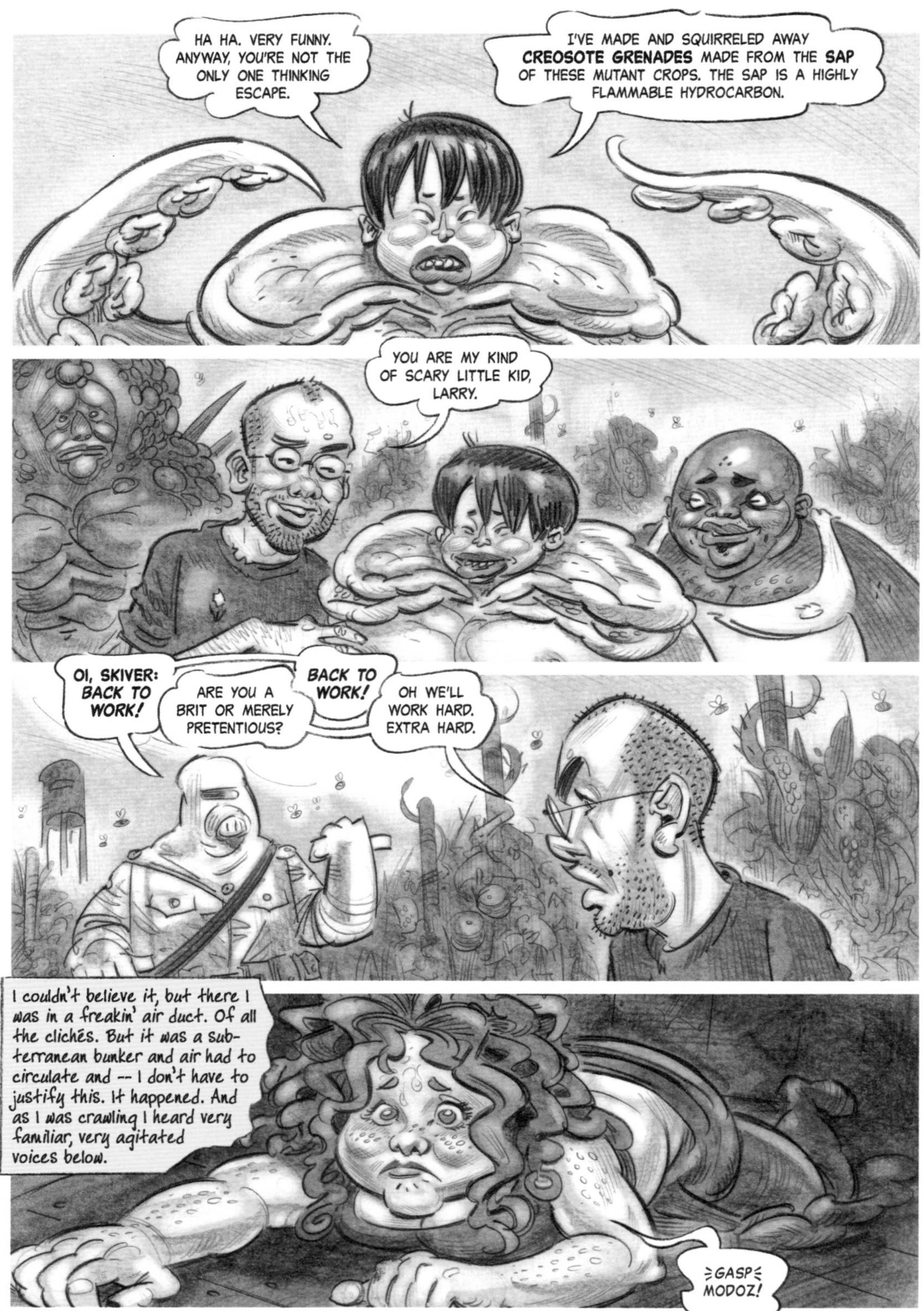
HA HA. VERY FUNNY. ANYWAY, YOU'RE NOT THE ONLY ONE THINKING ESCAPE.
I'VE MADE AND SQUIRRELED AWAY CREOSOTE GRENADES MADE FROM THE SAP OF THESE MUTANT CROPS. THE SAP IS A HIGHLY FLAMMABLE HYDROCARBON.
YOU ARE MY KIND OF SCARY LITTLE KID, LARRY.
OI, SKIVER: BACK TO WORK!
ARE YOU A BRIT OR MERELY PRETENTIOUS?
BACK TO WORK!
OH WE'LL WORK HARD. EXTRA HARD.
I couldn't believe it, but there I was in a freakin' air duct. Of all the clichés. But it was a subterranean bunker and air had to circulate and -- I don't have to justify this. It happened. And as I was crawling I heard very familiar, very agitated voices below.
GASP MODOZ!

THIS IS RI-GODDAMN-DICULOUS! YOU EUNUCHS APPEARING ON THE TELE-SCREENS! THAT'S MY JOB! THE CITIZENRY RESPECT MY REASSURING AUTHORITATIVE PRESENCE!
BUT, SIR, YOU'RE UNFIT TO APPEAR. THE PLEBS CAN'T SEE YOU LIKE THIS!
YOU THINK I DON'T KNOW THAT? PINHEAD! I'VE OUTGROWN THAT ROBO-SUIT! MAKE IT FIT!
IT'S NOT LIKE LETTING OUT SLACKS! WE NEED TO RETOOL, POSSIBLY BUILD ONE FROM SCRATCH.
SO DO IT! MAKE IT HAPPEN! FUCK IT! FUCKING THING SUCKS!
IT'S NOT AS EASY AS ALL THAT. THE ORIGINAL ENGINEERS ARE, UM, FOR LACK OF A BETTER WORD, DEAD.
DEAD? DEAD!?!
LOTS OF RECENT DEATHS. HALF THE POPULACE LOOKS A BIT, UM, CANCERISH? IT, UHHH, IT MIGHT BE THE, UM, MUTANT PRODUCE?
GREAT. IF THE BOMBS DIDN'T KILL 'EM THE CARROTS MIGHT.

KERRANG!
KLANG!
GUH
YAHH!
SPEAKING OF DEAD...
WE THANK YOU VERY SWEETLY FOR DOING IT SO NEATLY.
YOU'VE KILLED HIM SO COMPLETELY THAT WE THANK YOU VERY SWEETLY.
I'M NOT DEAD, YOU TOADYING PINHEADS! AND YOU--
ME? ME WHAT? LOOK AT YOU! YOU GUYS ARE ALL ALIKE: CONDEMN PUBLICLY WHAT YOU ARE PRIVATELY. YOU'RE WORSE THAN THOSE NEOCON TOILETHOMOS!

FUCK IT! TIME TO MEET YOUR PUBLIC, HEADFOOT O'BILEY!
OUCH! NO! NO! THEY CAN'T SEE ME LIKE THIS!
THEN I HAVE A BARGAINING CHIP. LET ME AND BOB AND WHOEVER WANTS TO LEAVE OUT OF THIS ZOO AND LET US ALONE!
BUT WE HAVE TO REPOPULATE!
WHY?
BECAUSE AMERICA HAS TO, UM... AND THE CHINESE AND AL-QAEDA AND... UH...
EXACTLY. YOU GOT NOTHIN'.
EWW. BUT YOU HAVE SOMETHING. DID YOU, UM, SOIL YOURSELF IN THE FALL?
EWW.

THEY'RE GONNA MISS ME BACK IN FOOD PREP.
BON COURAGE, MON AMI.
I DUNNO, GUYS. I DON'T THINK I CAN DO THIS. MAYBE A **SIT-IN** WOULD WORK? HALT PRODUCTION OF FOOD?
MISFITS
FOOD DROP
LISTEN, *CÉSAR CHÁVEZ*, WE'RE **NOT** FORMING A **UNION**, WE'RE DOING A **RESCUE AND ESCAPE**. WE HAVE **HOMEMADE GRENADES**. *VIVA LA REVOLUCIÓN!* ALL WE HAVE TO DO IS--
KK-KLANG!
--OH SHIT. SHOW TIME.
WE ARE **SO** GONNA GET DEAD, DUDE.

CHEERIO, CITIZEN FEMALE.
MICHELE?
SWEETIE, SWEETIE, SWEETIE!
AREN'T YOU HAPPY TO SEE ME? **THEY LET ME GO!**
B-BUT WE WERE COMING TO **RESCUE** YOU. WE MADE **GRENADES** AND EVERYTHING.
THAT'S **AWESOME** OF YOU, BUT **NO NEED**. I WAS GONNA **EXPOSE MODOZ**, BUT -- AND *DON'T WIG OUT* --

--I HAVE **THIS:**
THAT MAKES TWO OF US. FREAKY PEAS IN A POD.
SO, WE'RE **FREE TO GO?** JUST LIKE ***THAT?***
I GUESS SO. YOU SOUND DISAPPOINTED.
I, FOR ONE, AM RELIEVED AS SHIT, DUDE.
SO, WHAT DO WE DO NOW? HEAD BACK TO THE HONEY WAGONS?
I DUNNO. BUT WE CAN DO BETTER THAN THAT, I'M SURE.
AND WE DIDN'T EVEN GET TO BLOW ANYTHING UP.
LOOK AROUND YOU, KID. REDUNDANT MUCH?

AND THAT'S HOW IT HAPPENED. MAYBE IT'S ANTICLIMACTIC, BUT OUR STORY BEGAN WITH THE VERY BIGGEST OF BANGS AND ENDED NOT WITH A WHIMPER, BUT A DÉTENTE. MICHELE'S NEWFOUND MUTANT STATUS RENDERED HER OF NO USE TO MODOZ.
MICHELE WAS RIGHT, TOO: PLENTY IN THE BUNKER HAD THE SHEEP MENTALITY AND STAYED. ONLY A FEW FLED, SO IT WAS WIN/WIN FOR MODOZ -- WHO GOT TO KEEP HIS SLUGGY SECRET-- AND US.
WANNA HANG OUT WITH ANYONE TONIGHT? CINDY AND LENORE? KARL AND LYSA? BYRON?
MAYBE.
THE UNMUTATED HUMANS WERE ALREADY SHOWING SIGNS OF OBSOLESCENCE. THE PUKING. THE CANCER. OUR WORLD, WHICH HAD BEEN SO VERY CROWDED AND WAS NOW SO VERY SPACIOUS, HAD ROOM FOR ALL. IF THEY PREFERRED LIFE IN AN UNDERGROUND BUNKER LED BY A PUNDIT TURNED MOLLUSK, THEY WERE WELCOME TO IT. IF THEY COULD BREED, GOOD FOR THEM. TURNS OUT MUTANTS ARE STERILE. ALL THAT RADIATION, I GUESS.
IT'S HUMID TODAY. THINK IT'LL RAIN LATER?
MAYBE. LOOKS LIKE IT MIGHT.

≥YAWN≤ I'VE HAD ENOUGH POSING FOR THE DAY.
IT'S BEEN DECADES SINCE THE BOMBS FELL AND MICHELE AND I HAVEN'T AGED A DAY. NEITHER HAVE ANY OF OUR MUTANT BUDDIES. SADLY, THE SAME CAN'T BE SAID FOR OUR UNDEAD FRIENDS WHO EVENTUALLY ROTTED AWAY TO NOTHING. THREE PINK THINGS AND ALL, WE TOOK CAESAR IN. ED WAS RIGHT: HE *IS* A GOOD DOG.

OVER THE YEARS WE'VE BUILT A NICE HOME. WE'VE FORAGED FOR AND FOUND PRETTY MUCH EVERYTHING WE COULD DESIRE: BOOKS, FURNITURE, ART SUPPLIES. WE STILL GROW OUR FOOD AND LARRY-- *THAT FREAKY WIZARD*-- BUILT A REFINERY TO MAKE FUEL. CORN ETHANOL MIGHT'VE BEEN A BOONDOGGLE, BUT **MUTANT** CORN ETHANOL IS THE SHIT.

RELIGION GONE. POLITICS GONE. COMPUTERS GONE. LIFE IS GOOD.

WANNA PUT YOUR BRUSH DOWN, GO INSIDE AND HAVE SOME FUN?

LIFE IS *VERY, VERY* GOOD.

"The apocalypse is coming. That's the one thing I like about George Bush. I really think he can get us into the fucking apocalypse, like the biblical — I really think he believes that he will be the guy, you know, in the white hat." — Patton Oswalt, ***Feelin' Kinda Patton***

Afterword

The genesis of ***From the Ashes*** was simple enough, sort of.

There are two subjects to which I am very attracted and keep returning: zombies and the man-made post-apocalypse. I think a lot of it comes down to my misanthropy. Don't get me wrong. I love my friends and family and most especially you, my dear reader. *You* are tops. But the notion of this planet's load being lightened by a few billion-odd souls is not without its charms. Of course, zombies still clutter the joint up, but the apocalypse. Oh mama, that's a regular clearing-house. Generally, I enjoy making light of these themes, but I have been known to get serious. My forthcoming (shameless plug) novel, ***Pariah***, is much more serious than most of my published work (out July 2010). It boasts oceans of the undead, so Earth is still crowded. I did another humorous post-apocalypse comic a number of years ago called ***Monkey Jank***, for *Penthouse Comix*. It was about two "normal" (re: not mutated) human females on the prowl for sex with non-mutated men. Yes, a strip about comely lasses who couldn't get laid done for La Casa Guccione. It was *not* popular with the higher-ups, who unsurprisingly axed it. Still, I had fun doing it.

Anyway, ***From the Ashes***. You've read the book, presumably (unless you're one of those weirdoes who watch the bonus material before the movie, not having seen it prior, in which case, what is your damage, weirdo?), so you know I am a news junkie in recovery. I became a freak for it during the previous administration's reign and believe me, eight years of Bush-flavored current events put me in touch with a part of my psyche that had lain dormant for many years: the part that considers *The End of the World* a credible, even plausible notion.

Recently, my fears that Bush might indeed have envisaged himself as *The Bringer of the Bible-Style End of Days* were vindicated. Former president of France Jacques Chirac revealed that in the run-up to the invasion of Iraq, Bush had contacted him and told him: "Gog and Magog are at work in the Middle East...The biblical prophecies are being fulfilled...This confrontation is willed by God, who wants to use this conflict to erase his people's enemies before a New Age begins." (Council for Secular Humanism, August 6th, 2009)

That *should* be 31 flavors of WTF, only it's no surprise given what a bible-thumping thingamaboob Dubya is. I'm not sure what kind of "New Age" Bush was blathering about, but I'm sure he didn't mean the kind that scintillates with tie-dye, vortexes and expensive crystals (which, actually, would be quite annoying). Still, Gog and Magog get a name-check in this book, so I'm proud of that.

Anyway, back to my visions of gloom and doom. In a way, I give terrorists a pass. It's their job, after all, to instill terror. Mission accomplished, boys; well done. But my own government? For fuck's sake, they were supposed to assuage my dread. As the clock ticked down on Bush's second term my anxiety over what he might do as a fare-thee-well to the citizens of the world grew. As a good soldier of the Lord, could he bring on The Rapture?

I started work in earnest on ***From the Ashes*** in July 2008. Plenty of time left for me to sweat about Bush letting the Big One rip. I decided to set it prior to the election, not only because I didn't want to be too topical (that dates badly), but also didn't really want to assign blame for The End on either candidate (or, as you've read, even Bush; better to let the cause be a bit mysterious).

The night Obama was declared victor I felt like I was released from the world's tightest corset. I didn't view Obama as some kind of messianic savior, but he was clearly a marked improvement. I liked that he was eloquent without being stuffy. I liked that he was young. I liked that it seems probable he and his missus still knock boots. A well-laid president is less likely to want to end the world, as is one with young children whose future might actually mean something to him. And knowing that under all that heavenly glow he was first and foremost a *politician*, he couldn't disappoint me too much because they *all* have feet of clay—even the good ones. Still, optimism was the vibe.

And there was the rub.

I began to worry that maybe a comic about nuclear obliteration would be hopelessly out of sync. Well, no need to fret about relevance. Iran's nascent nuclear program stirs the worry pot, especially the recent revelation it's "perfected the technology to create and detonate a nuclear warhead and is merely awaiting the word from its Supreme Leader, Ayatollah Ali Khamenei, to produce its first bomb." (*London Times*, August 3rd, 2009) Lines like, "North Korea today warned it would use nuclear weapons in a 'merciless offensive' if provoked, two weeks after testing a Hiroshima-size device." (*The Guardian*, June 9th, 2009) make ***From the Ashes*** fresh as, well, today's headlines.

So.

The other thing was comics. Or "graphic novels," a term that becomes less and less an accurate descriptor by the moment. These days, it seems the bulk of "graphic novels" —at least ones released by mainstream book publishers—would more accurately be billed "graphic memoirs" or "graphic non-fiction." There's nothing wrong with either, but novels they ain't.

The phrase "speculative memoir" popped into my head and that, combined with all my real-world dread, sparked this baby up. Maybe Cormac McCarthy wanted to take all the fun out of the end of the world (I've still yet to read ***The Road***, but I gather it's not a laugh-a-thon), but I aimed to bring it back. After all, you can't make a post-apocalyptic omelet without killing a few billion people and mutating a goodly portion of the rest. But that's as it should be. A post-apocalypse without mutants is like a day without sunshine. Plus, after nearly 20 years together, I'd yet to feature my amazing wife, Michele. She's endured nearly two decades of me, so to her the apocalypse would be a piece of cake.

So, that's it. I love Michele and I love the apocalypse (my version of it, anyway; the real thing not so much). Like Reese's Pieces, two great tastes tasting great together (as opposed to ***Recess Pieces***, my zombies vs. tykes graphic novel, which is still available so order yours now!). I hope you enjoyed spending some quality time in my nuked-out world. And as a reward, here's the bonus section, an assortment of preparatory art that led to making this book. Thanks for reading this and stay tuned.

Bob Fingerman
New York, NY, September 2009

POCKALIPS

These are a couple of the first sketches I did of us in the post-apocalyptic setting.

It was crucial to me that the art in this book be freer than any I'd done before. Though there's nothing wrong with ink, I came to see in my own work that much of the vitality of my pencil drawing was leeched away by my inks. For years I've striven towards finished work that felt as fresh as my sketchy stuff. I think I'm getting there with the work in ***From the Ashes***.

Note the lettering above the drawing. ***Pockalips*** was a possible title. But then I realized it sounded fuckin' retarded.

There's a tendency in cartoonists to either over-prettify or over-uglify ourselves when we use ourselves as protagonist. Michele is lovable and cute, but I didn't want to make myself too handsome or too grotesque. Thing is, I lack objectivity. So, look at my author photo and you decide. I was also wrasslin' with how distorted the cartooning was going to be. I look a bit like an Easter Island head here. Can't be having that.

Vanity, thy name is Bob.

When first shopping ***From the Ashes*** I decided to do a bunch of drawings to give prospective editors an idea of what the art would look like. It was also to help me get in the mindset and figure out how I wanted this sucker to look. These warm-ups helped land it at IDW.

Though not exactly Harlequin fodder, *romance* was an element I wanted to make clear. I didn't want ***From the Ashes*** to be goopy and saccharine, but the way I feel about Michele is integral to the plot, so some lovey-dovey sketching was in order. That my hand is cupping some cheekage is merely in keeping with how I normally show my affection. Sue me, the world just ended.

This cheery, if somewhat feeble-looking, mutant didn't make it into the book, though I'm not sure why. Looking at this sketch I think it might've been an oversight. He's got that certain indefinable something. "It," if you will. Those buboes. Those swollen feet. He's a dishy little number.

By the way, the type on Michele's shirt isn't some mean-spirited commentary on my part. Michele actually has this long-sleeve tee from Juicy Couture that she got as a giveaway at a party they threw. I don't remember how or why she was there, but I like that shirt, so that's why I dressed her that way.

Cannibalism was always on the menu for my apocalypse. I hear it's also in ***The Road***, but I bet mine is funnier. I find "foodies" pretty unbearable. Then again, I often find food to be a bit of a grind. Some people fantasize about giving up sleep to get more out of the day, but I'd keep sleep and forgo eating.

In addition to mutants, the undead were always going to be part of my PA landscape (that's post-apocalypse, not Pennsylvania, though we all know Pittsburgh is home of the modern zombie). I didn't want them to be scary flesh-eaters, though. In fact, I figured they wouldn't eat anything.

I'm not quite sure what's up with those poses on the bottom. Michele kind of looks like a stiffly posed doll and I look like I'm limbering up for a crack at ***DJ Hero***.™

More trial runs at how I'd draw us. For a while I toyed with the idea of going the Japanese "super deformed" route. Not quite, but almost. Stubbier proportions to make the art cuter, sort of as a way to mitigate the awfulness of the apocalyptic setting. I still went with a bit of compacting, but cutesy isn't really my thing.

Not only have I absorbed hours and hours of nauseating video of "Rile O'Biley" performing his dark magic, but I had to draw him myriad times.

Above is my first stab at putting his countenance down on paper and one of my best, I think. He's oddly beatified, hence my note, "too kindly." But one of his dark gifts is that he *can* look kindly from time to time.

Byron was always going to have goat eyes and tentacles (and a crisp pleat in his trousers), but the rest of him took longer to figure out, as these pages show.

Cindy the humpback made her first appearance on this humble wee Post-it® note.

These are the complete thumbnails for Chapter 1, including cover ideas. Thumbnailing, while essential, is my least favorite part of the process.

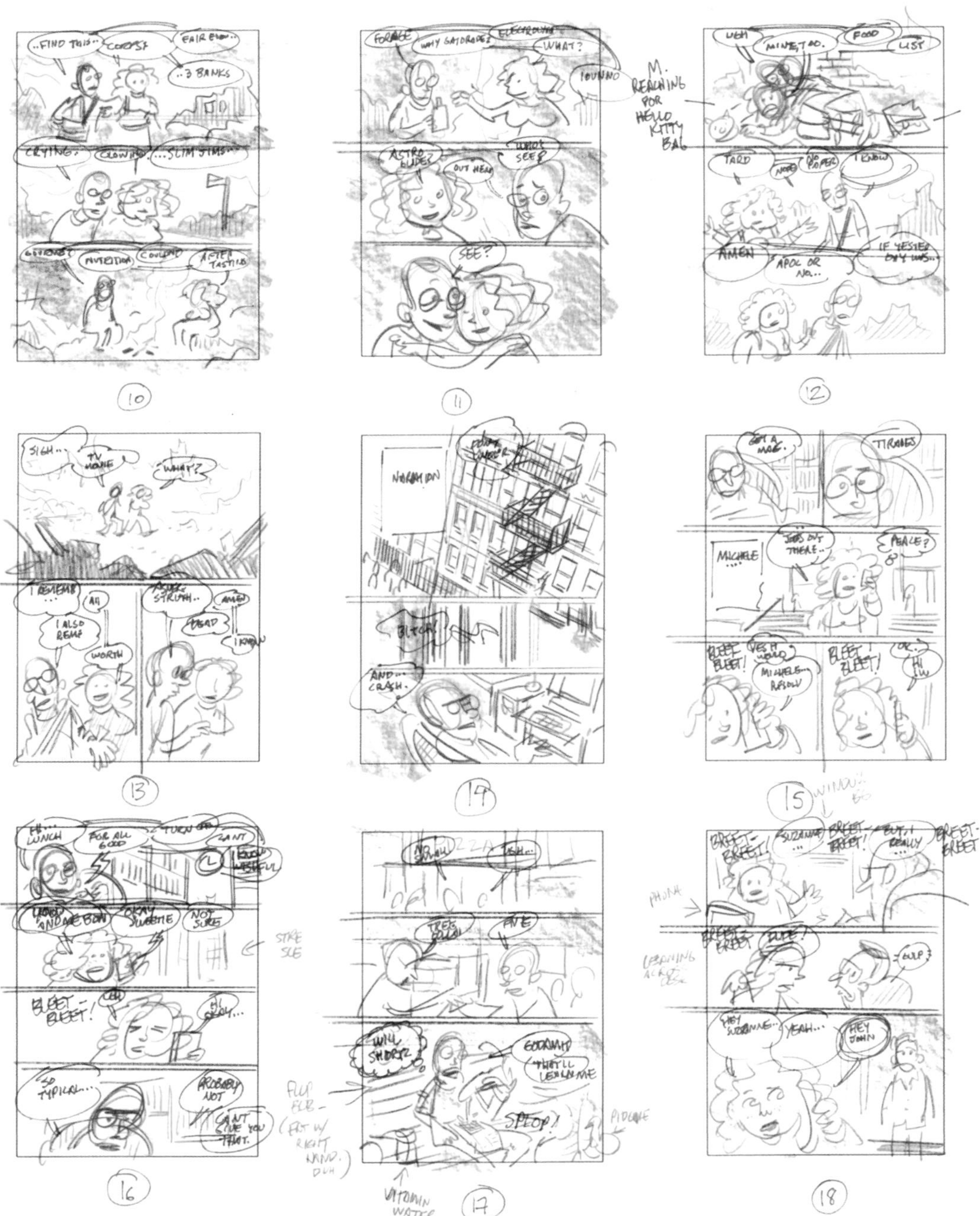
..FIND THIS..
..3 BANKS
CRYING
NUTRITION
10
WHY GATORADE?
WHAT?
IDUNNO
ASTRO GLIDE?
OUT HERE
SEE?
11
M. REACHING FOR HELLO KITTY BAG
UGH
FOOD
LIST
TARD
I KNOW
AMEN
APOL OR NO...
12
SIGH...
TV MOVIE
WHAT?
AH
I ALSO REMEMB
WORTH
AMEN
DEAD
I KNOW
13
NARRATION
AND... CRASH.
14
MICHELE...
PEACE?
BLEET BLEET!
BLEET BLEET!
15
FOR ALL GOOD
NOT SURE
SO TYPICAL...
PROBABLY NOT
CAN'T GIVE YOU THAT.
16
FINE
SPLOP!
VITAMIN WATER
17
SUZANNE...
BUT, I REALLY ...
PHONE
GULP?
HEY SUZANNE...
YEAH...
HEY JOHN
18

AM I FIRED?
I...
KNOW WHAT?
JOHN
PLEASE!
X-CLOSE UP
DON'T REMIND
UH-HOH...
I HAVE TO
TIP-TAP-TAP-TIP!
BYE.
AT HILL BOTTOM
THUD!
OUCH
BUT IT COULD
DON'T BE SILLY
19
20
21
SINISTER, SHADOWY FIGURES EATING
OH MY GOD
GOOD ENOUGH
23 IS CANNIBAL SPLASH
YEAH MORE
OBVIOUSLY
BONES
CANNIBAL HORDE...
CONT'D
YAWN
FROM THE ASHES
22
24
FTA #1 COVER IDEAS
UPC
FROM THE ASHES
FROM THE ASHES
FROM THE ASHES
huh
HAPPY/ FROLICKING
CARPET OF SKELETONS & DEAD BODIES

Here are thumbnails for covers from the series, four of which passed muster and went to finish.

Opposite and beyond: covers from the individual issues.

yawn...

TRASH

TRASH

©
2009

TELERANGER

Addendum

This drawing is here to make amends for the fact that this malignant crybaby didn't make it into the book. That is totally my bad, so this in some tiny way redresses that foolish oversight. He should have been wandering the wastelands, naked and afraid (like he does backstage, before every taping of his show).

For more about this book and its creator:
http://fromtheashescomic.blogspot.com/
and
http://bobfingerman.com/

Also by Bob Fingerman

GRAPHIC NOVELS
(you know, comics)

Minimum Wage
White Like She
Beg the Question
You Deserved It
Recess Pieces

NOVELS
(you know, the regular
kind *without* pictures)

Bottomfeeder
Pariah

ILLUSTRATED NOVELLA
(okay, this one is really weird
and hard to categorize)

Connective Tissue